UNDERSTANDING ALICE McDERMOTT

UNDERSTANDING CONTEMPORARY AMERICAN LITERATURE
Matthew J. Bruccoli, Founding Editor
Linda Wagner-Martin, Series Editor

Also of Interest

Understanding Alice Adams, Bryant Mangum
Understanding Anne Tyler, Alice Hall Petry
Understanding Irène Némirovsky, Margaret Scanlan
Understanding Iris Murdoch, Cheryl K. Bove
Understanding Jane Smiley, Neil Nakadate
Understanding Jill McCorkle, Barbara Bennett
Understanding Lee Smith, Danielle N. Johnson
Understanding Marge Piercy, Donna M. Bickford
Understanding Marilynne Robinson, Alex Engebretson
Understanding Penelope Fitzgerald, Peter Wolfe

UNDERSTANDING ALICE McDERMOTT

Margaret Hallissy

Published by the University of South Carolina Press
Columbia, South Carolina 29208

www.sc.edu/uscpress

Manufactured in the United States of America

29 28 27 26 25 24 23 22 21 20
10 9 8 7 6 5 4 3 2 1

Library of Congress Cataloging-in-Publication Data
can be found at http://catalog.loc.gov/.

ISBN 978-1-64336-027-0 (hardback)
ISBN 978-1-64336-028-7 (ebook)

To my family
past, present, and future

. . . everything I know is memory or story or hope.

A Bigamist's Daughter

CONTENTS

SERIES EDITOR'S PREFACE

The Understanding Contemporary American Literature series was founded by the estimable Matthew J. Bruccoli (1931–2008), who envisioned these volumes as guides or companions for students as well as good nonacademic readers, a legacy that will continue as new volumes are developed to fill in gaps among the nearly one hundred series volumes published to date and to embrace a host of new writers only now making their marks on our literature.

As Professor Bruccoli explained in his preface to the volumes he edited, because much influential contemporary literature makes special demands, "the word *understanding* in the titles was chosen deliberately. Many willing readers lack an adequate understanding of how contemporary literature works; that is, of what the author is attempting to express and the means by which it is conveyed." Aimed at fostering this understanding of good literature and good writers, the criticism and analysis in the series provide instruction in how to read certain contemporary writers—explicating their material, language, structures, themes, and perspectives—and facilitate a more profitable experience of the works under discussion.

In the twenty-first century Professor Bruccoli's prescience gives us an avenue to publish expert critiques of significant contemporary American writing. The series continues to map the literary landscape and to provide both instruction and enjoyment. Future volumes will seek to introduce new voices alongside canonized favorites, to chronicle the changing literature of our times, and to remain, as Professor Bruccoli conceived, contemporary in the best sense of the word.

Linda Wagner-Martin, Series Editor

CHAPTER 1

Understanding Alice McDermott

Like many of her characters, Alice McDermott was born in one of New York City's outer boroughs, Brooklyn, in 1953, to an Irish American Catholic family. She and her two brothers were raised in Elmont, New York, just east of the Queens border in southwest Nassau County on Long Island. McDermott's early education took place in the Roman Catholic school system, St. Boniface Elementary School in Elmont and Sacred Heart Academy in Hempstead, from which she graduated in 1971. While McDermott was studying for her bachelor's degree at the State University of New York at Oswego, Paul Briand, the instructor of a course in nonfiction writing, identified his young student's gift. As McDermott would tell the story, "he called me down after class and said as he straightened papers and packed his briefcase, 'I've got bad news for you, kid. You're a writer. You'll never shake it.' Handing me my career."[1] Her next step, after graduating from Oswego in 1975, was a master's degree, earned in 1978 at the University of New Hampshire. There another great teacher, Mark Smith, saw potential in a draft of what would become her first novel, *A Bigamist's Daughter.* Smith put McDermott in touch with the esteemed literary agent Harriet Wasserman, who in turn recommended her work to Jonathan Galassi at Houghton Mifflin, later at Random House. Galassi took a chance on this then-unknown writer and offered her a contract based on the unfinished manuscript. McDermott tells the story of this promising start to her career with characteristic modesty; as she phrased it in an interview with Diane Osen, "It had very little to do with me . . . it was simply good fortune."[2] But these early mentors were professional judges of literary talent, and the young Alice clearly had it.

A Bigamist's Daughter was considered to hold great promise—a promise fulfilled in that each of her successive novels was nominated for or received prestigious literary awards while also appealing to a general readership. McDermott's fourth novel, *Charming Billy,* received the National Book Award for Fiction in 1998 and the American Book Award in 1999. Her most recent novel, *The Ninth Hour,* was published in 2017 to stellar reviews. After stints as teacher and writer-in-residence at various American institutions, including the University of New Hampshire, the University of California at San Diego, and American University, she currently holds the position of Richard A. Macksey Professor for Distinguished Teaching in the Humanities at the Writing Seminars of Johns Hopkins University. In this role she has been an effective instructor and mentor, according to former students and successful novelists Chimamanda Ngozi Adichie, author of *Purple Hibiscus, Americanah,* and others; and Matthew Thomas, author of *We Are Not Ourselves.*[3] Married to David Armstrong, a neuroscientist, and the mother of three adult children, McDermott lives in Bethesda, Maryland.

While McDermott's literary reputation rests mainly on her novels, she has also published a distinguished body of short fiction and essays that introduce or recapitulate recurrent themes in her longer fiction. As a book reviewer, McDermott mainly reviews novels resembling her own in some way, such as fiction focusing on the inner lives of women and girls as well as fiction for children and for young adults, especially in small, insular communities like the Long Island suburbs featured in her own work. Similarly, fiction of the Irish American Catholic experience is a logical area in which McDermott's expertise as a reviewer is sought.

Alice McDermott keeps her family life private, but she has often commented on her professional life and her religious life. Regarding her writing, her responses are often characterized by what interviewer Wendy Smith calls her "diffidence" and what McDermott herself calls, in the same interview, her "sense of apology: Look, I'm not going to waste your time."[4] With rave reviews of her most recent novel, *The Ninth Hour,* McDermott is at the peak of her career, yet still she seems unduly modest about the extent of her success, as if writing first-rate fiction were possible for anyone who set her mind to it. From her earliest days as a writer, at a time when women were inclined to downplay the domestic side of their lives for fear of not being taken seriously, she has apparently sensed no particular conflict between her life as wife and mother and her life as writer. In 1992 McDermott presented herself as a typical mom, describing her writing schedule as tied to her housekeeping and child care responsibilities. Her office at the time was located "right through the laundry room, so I can always think of other things that need to be done!"[5] In 1998, by which time she had completed her first four novels, including *Charming Billy,* her three children were still small, and she felt comfortable telling an interviewer that she shaped her writing time around their school schedule.[6] This matter-of-fact approach to her writing may be a residue of the sort of humility encouraged in young Irish American Catholic girls of her generation, but it has served her well in terms of literary productivity. There may be laundry to do, but there are award-winning novels to write as well, and her attitude seems to be that she will just get on with it. As she said in a lecture at her alma mater, Sacred Heart Academy in Hempstead, in 2017, writing is a "9 to 5 job for me," the main element of which is, in her words, "being there."

Voice, Language, Memory

Understanding Alice McDermott requires paying close attention to three key elements: voice, language, and memory. The concept of voice—the sense of being in the mind of a unique person—is all-important to her fiction, and in her book reviews she often uses the successful creation of a distinct voice as a litmus test of literary achievement. One challenge she poses to herself is to give voice to people who are neither highly educated nor sophisticated, yet they deal with ultimate questions that have been the stuff of theological and philosophical debate for centuries. This, like everything else in her fiction, is consistent with the religious beliefs McDermott expresses in interviews and essays. McDermott's characters—whether a high school graduate who works for Con Edison, a housewife, a teenage babysitter—all must work out their salvation in as serious a manner as the greatest philosopher. But they will think with a different vocabulary and speak in a different voice.

These characters' intellectual toolkit consists almost exclusively of the language of Roman Catholicism. Another tribe might speak in terms of Marxism, or of Freudian psychoanalysis, or of mythology, but not McDermott's people. Her characters have not been introduced to these alternative thought systems, which would normally happen via higher education. Catholicism provides them with their first and only language, "a vocabulary that they might not otherwise have."[7] This is true even if they are, as she is, disappointed in the institutional Church. McDermott explains how her characters continue to employ the language of faith even when faith itself falters. In her view, "The moral collapse of the institutional Catholic Church—via the priest abuse scandal—has left me, and many Catholics of my generation, I think, sifting through the ruins. . . . in my case the search for what remains valuable focusses on language itself: Catholic prayer, ritual, the naming of things."[8] These elements of Catholic language, discovered among the "ruins," provide a unifying principle within and between McDermott's works.

In passage after passage in her fiction, the rituals of the Catholic tradition provide significant detail, and details of churchgoing in particular create a believable Catholic microcosm. In a 1997 essay, "The Annual Sermon, Retold," McDermott describes a sermon preached during "the last Mass on Christmas Day" as "a challenge for any priest. . . . The congregation at this hour was made up mostly of parents with young children, hung-over teenagers and silver-haired retirees who hoped to avoid the crush of the earlier, more elaborate Christmas services." The essence of ritual is repetition, but repetition can be boring. McDermott senses the priest's exhausted search for something new in the Christmas story, a "narrative, of character and plot . . . a story told and re-told." In a moment of inspiration, the priest asks the congregants to "consider this": "The Creator made human. Come among us as a child. . . . A child's birth. . . . A young mother's love. God, the First Cause, come among us." This simple language, she concludes, is "sermon enough."[9] Listening with the mind of a writer and teacher, she silently applauds the priest's instinct to do what she tries to do in her writing, what she has often insisted that her students do in theirs: get to the point, then quit. For McDermott, who in 2003 would call herself the "lunatic in the pew," the sermon becomes a writing lesson as well as an occasion of spiritual enlightenment.

Small details of domestic rituals can also trigger insights of larger religious significance. In her 1998 essay "Night without End, Amen," a window fan—hardly a typical object of religious veneration—serves as a metaphor for the influence of Catholic ways of thinking on her family's childrearing practices. This detail of her family's life, this fan, situates them as to economics and social class (they were not among the pioneers of domestic air conditioning), as to beliefs about gender roles (the undisturbed sleep of fathers, the bread-winners, was considered more important than that of mothers). The fan also provides an insight into the Catholic mindset. That single window fan, blowing hot air into and around in an already stifling house, illustrates the Catholic assumption that suffering is inevitable and must be borne patiently: "we prepared for heat the way we were being prepared for life: with ritual and doctrine, and the faithful adherence to formula."

Writing this essay many years after, remembering the penitential summer heat of her childhood, causes McDermott to associate it with other hot nights—after the prom, meeting her husband, holding a new baby—and to note how these associations become "part of the childhood memory" of the window fan.[10] Memory—especially its recursive nature, with new memories added to old ones and old ones adapted to new realities—is in fact the main structural principle of her writing. In a 1998 interview she describes what she calls the "real parallel between fiction-writing and memory," especially memory as affected by the passage of time. For any given real-life event, memory involves re-creation of the event over time. This makes us "all editors of our own past."[11] McDermott's characters often return in memory to the key stories of their lives, retell them, and in the retelling, re-create the narrative, thus taking on what she describes as a circular structure.

Speaking of *Charming Billy* in particular, McDermott explains the correlation between memory and structure thus:

> Now, as soon as you have a collective memory you have various versions of it; and as soon as you have a collective memory over time you have conjecture, because over time what we think may have happened, or what we assume to have happened, becomes as much a part of our memory as those things that were clearly and absolutely observed. None of us, in relating stories, sticks to the facts. So the circling of the structure of the novel was very much a part of that convergence of retelling and imagining.[12]

This passage is key to understanding the remembered material in McDermott's novels. There is often a central story to which characters return in memory, with each retelling or remembrance of the story contributing a significant detail or two to the narrative.

Memory also accounts for another important element of McDermott's writing style: repetition. Words and phrases recur in memory, many of them the verbal fragments of Catholic prayer learned in childhood, impossible to forget, occasionally cropping up at inappropriate times. Bits and pieces of Catholic life are scattered throughout her novels: Calvary Cemetery in Queens, Bishop Fulton J. Sheen's television program, high school uniforms, the lives of various saints, the sacraments, Christmas and Easter, fragments of hymns, incense. All of these, to paraphrase a repeated phrase from *At Weddings and Wakes,* are part of everything her characters know. McDermott's novels are not merely concerned with the trappings of faith, however, but with its essential beliefs.

The Reluctant Catholic

In McDermott's essays on her religious beliefs, she acknowledges, somewhat ruefully, that Catholicism is considered at best quaint, at worst delusional, in many contemporary circles. She knows how far her (sometimes "reluctant," in her word) Catholicism is from the mainstream of modern intellectual life and how far the Catholic Church as an institution has fallen from its own professed ideals. Nevertheless, several important essays and interviews are devoted, in an informal, sometimes even humorous way, to what theologians call apologetics, a branch of religious studies devoted to the defense of the faith. Derived from the Latin *apologia,* the theological term does not have the connotation of shamefacedness included in its modern form, but it does connote more certainty than McDermott can claim to possess. By 2013, in "Redeemed from

Death? The Faith of a Catholic Novelist," although McDermott has come to embrace the identity of the "Catholic novelist," she is at the same time far from steadfast in her faith (hence the question mark). Even as she reaffirms her membership in the Catholic Church, she also admits that she has doubts about its central tenet, the immortality of the soul. Her "faith in this magical thinking, this Glorious Impossible, comes and goes. It compels me and comforts me as much as it fills me with skepticism and doubt."[13]

Her faith may waver, but the influence of her religion on her fiction does not. The language of Catholicism is retained, and so is the sacramental vision. Just as the story of a window fan is really about coping with suffering, so other everyday objects reflect the supernatural. In an interview with Paul Contino, McDermott defines the Catholic concept of sacrament thus: "an outward sign elevated into something else, the ordinary made into occasions of grace."[14] This is an orthodox definition, its wording hewing closely to that memorized by Catholic children in preparation for their own sacraments. The sacramental view of the world is that supernatural significance inheres in all things, and this is also an artistic principle for McDermott. She observes that "the artist . . . takes the ordinary, finite, daily stuff of our condition and shapes and reshapes it until it goes beyond itself, until it yields a larger meaning."[15] In this sacramental view of art, water, for example, is not only water but a sign of the cleansing power of God's love.

This same sacramental view of the world is chronicled in her 2010 essay "Revelation," in which an ordinary experience leads to a spiritual insight. McDermott's mother and her mother's friends, all residents in an assisted living home, are enthralled with a story about Jesus's mother, Mary, which, they believe, is in the Book of Revelations. According to the ladies' version of the story, Mary went, after the birth of Jesus, "into the desert, to a place God had prepared for her." Variants of this phrase, repeated over and over in the essay, constitute a meditation on the (possibly apocryphal) story. Ever the sarcastic teenager in her interactions with her mother, McDermott does not believe that the Book of Revelations should be taken literally, and says so, describing it as the locus of "visionary, end-of-days stuff." But because this story brings such comfort to the old ladies, "here at their own end of days," the revelation is that storytelling is more important to faith than doctrine is.

Inevitably, then, Catholicism is an essential principle of continuity linking all her writings. The faith, she says, is

> not only a means to an end in my fiction but an essential part of my own understanding of the world. In my own understanding of the world, the authority and truth of the human heart revealed again and again our

> insatiable longing to prove that we will not be trumped by death, that our spirits endure, that our love for one another endures, and it is because of our love for one another that our hearts most [*sic*] rail against meaninglessness.[16]

Fiction and faith are one. "This is my material, this is the story I have chosen to tell, this is the language I must use . . . this is mine, inevitably, and I am obliged only to make the best of it. . . . Resignation and delight: I am a Catholic after all."[17]

The Cast of Characters

Important as Catholicism is to McDermott, McDermott cannot be pigeonholed only as a Catholic novelist. Critical attention thus far has discussed McDermott as an ethnic novelist as well. According to Paul Gray, "Alice McDermott has staked an impressive claim on a subject matter and a turf—Irish-American Catholic families congregated, for the most part, in New York City and its suburbs on Long Island."[18] Her characters' Catholic connection manifests itself in a variety of ways: as a collection of tribal folkways; as an anchor in a turbulent world; as a prison; as a pervasive sense of the sacred innate in and manifested through the mundane. Their Irish connection provides them with a set of beliefs and practices tying them to a treasured but often poorly understood heritage. They are also the carriers of traits specific to their location, both in space and on the social ladder. They are outer-borough New Yorkers, or residents of the adjacent counties on Long Island, usually working in lower-middle-class jobs and living in modest homes; they are members of families. As a group, they are remarkably stationary; few of them venture far from their island home. McDermott's precise description of this fictional environment situates her characters also. Within the parameters of social class and their largely self-imposed geographical restrictions, in small city apartments and modest suburban houses, in churches and schools, on subways and buses, on beaches and in summer cottages of the less-prestigious towns on Long Island's East End, the characters experience the full range of human emotion: love and loss, the pull of the past, the power of memory.

Virtually all of McDermott's characters operate within a web of family relationships: dutiful daughters and wayward sons, overworked parents of young children, overbearing matriarchs of failure-to-launch adult children, black sheep, drunks. Key *dramatis personae* also include Irish emigrants carrying the baggage of memory across the ocean. Catholic nuns and priests, spoiled and unspoiled, populate the pages. Some of the characters' problems result from their efforts to abide by the stringent rules of their faith. McDermott's typical character has a job, not a career, and is incompletely educated, confined socially and professionally as well as geographically. Narrative voices can be single or multiple, incorporating several versions of any given event. Important facts are sometimes unknown, sometimes deliberately suppressed; interpretations of events are subjective and self-justifying; all these factors shape the narrator's (or narrators') ability to tell a story that is certain and true.

McDermott revisits her signature elements in each novel (religion, Long Island, being Irish), but each novel is also unique in the way it develops these elements and adds new ones. Therefore, each chapter herein builds on the one before. In *A Bigamist's Daughter,* McDermott introduces the consistent setting for all her novels and most of her short fiction: Long Island, including the outer boroughs of New York City, Brooklyn and Queens. This novel also focuses considerable attention on the process of writing fiction, a subject to which McDermott returns in her essays and interviews but not in her fiction thus far. *That Night* is a tale of suburbia that also picks up a theme introduced in *A Bigamist's Daughter,* the Catholic belief in the immortality of the soul. *At Weddings and Wakes,* the most Irish-influenced of all her novels to date, focuses on the emigrant experience and the uneasy path to assimilation. McDermott's best-known novel, *Charming Billy,* explores a typically Catholic mode of thought: the sacramental view of the world that sees all material things as emblematic of spiritual realities. *Child of My Heart* is on the surface a coming-of-age novel tracing the events of a single summer in the life of a young Long Island girl; on a deeper level, it is a meditation on mortality. *After This* is centered on the physicality of women's lives and the innate spirituality of those lives. In all of her novels, McDermott uses clear sensory imagery to convey her themes; this technique is most obvious in *Someone.* McDermott's most recent novel, *The Ninth Hour,* returns to her characteristic themes but with a moral and theological ambiguity unexpected in a novel about that most traditional of religious groups, Roman Catholic nuns. Finally, each of McDermott's uncollected stories contributes to an understanding of her novels and forms a coherent body of work. The full bibliography includes all of McDermott's writing, including essays and book reviews, as well as scholarly articles and chapters and selected reviews of her novels.

CHAPTER 2

A Bigamist's Daughter (1982)

First novels are often at least partially autobiographical, and this is true of *A Bigamist's Daughter.* Briefly, after graduating from college, Alice McDermott worked for a vanity press in a position even more humble than that the one she assigns to Elizabeth Connolly, the novel's protagonist. How McDermott came to work at a vanity press is itself an Irish American Catholic story. In interviews, McDermott often notes that a writing career was not among the range of possibilities presented to her in her youth. Her parents, she says, though committed to education, were less than enthusiastic about her becoming a writer; they "saw me starving in a garret and tried to steer me away from it the same way they tried to steer me away from cocaine: 'I know it sounds very appealing right now, but believe me, you'll regret it!'"[1] In the Brooklyn/Queens/Long Island setting of McDermott's upbringing—and that of her characters, even in the 1980s in which the novel is set—a young Catholic girl would likely have been steered toward an undemanding job that would hold her over until marriage, or provide a fallback should the marriage, or the husband, fail. A woman's work was definitely not imagined as a career, the assumption being that life as a wife and mother would provide fulfillment enough. After all, Grace Kelly, that apotheosis of Irish American Catholic womanhood, vanished from films after marrying Prince Rainier of Monaco in 1956. So McDermott's parents were not unusual in suggesting that the young Alice should attend the Katharine Gibbs School, founded in 1911, which "once set the gold standard for glorified secretaries."[2] Post-Gibbs, her parents advised, "you can get a good job in publishing if you have your secretarial skills. Then maybe you can be an editor and if you really want to write, you can write at night. But you'll have health insurance!"[3]

McDermott went to college instead of secretarial school, but thereafter, as if unconsciously following her parents' advice, worked briefly at a press similar to Vista, in a job for which a scretarial-school education would have been adequate. McDermott remembers the Katie Gibbs episode with her typical humor and dedicates *A Bigamist's Daughter* to her parents. Her time at the vanity press provided her with intricate details of the industry as well as reflections on the writing process. Other continuing concerns are introduced in *A Bigamist's Daughter:* the geography of Long Island, the Irish American Catholic experience, and the nature of storytelling. Specific to this novel is the emphasis on duplicity/duality/duplication: the many and intersecting ways in which the characters dupe each other and themselves.

Coming Attractions: The Overture

Like its successors, *A Bigamist's Daughter* is set in a limited geographical area: Manhattan, known to Long Islanders as "the city," as if the only one; the outer boroughs, Brooklyn and Queens, across the East River on Long Island; and the two counties, Nassau and Suffolk, east of Brooklyn and Queens on the same island. For locals, the distance between Manhattan and either Brooklyn or Queens is measured not in the length of the bridges and tunnels that connect them but in the social and psychological differences that consign Brooklyn and Queens residents to a status decidedly below Manhattanites in any conceivable pecking order, even in the bridge-and-tunnel crowd's own estimation. Elizabeth's mother, a Brooklynite, may have been more likely to fall in love because she met her future husband, the future bigamist, at "a party. Park Avenue, very posh" (*BD* 85); implicit in this comment is "posh compared to Brooklyn." And the distance between Queens and Brooklyn and "the Island," Nassau and Suffolk, like the distance between the boroughs and the city, is measured in increased affluence and higher social class more than in miles.

Subtle details in *A Bigamist's Daughter* highlight McDermott's intimate knowledge of local geography and lore and serve as an introduction to the Long Island settings that will appear in future novels. Elizabeth's mother's friend, for example, is killed in an auto accident on Queens Boulevard, a notoriously dangerous multilane urban thoroughfare that locals call, with grim humor, the "Boulevard of Death." Regarding Calvary Cemetery, a huge Catholic necropolis just off Queens Boulevard, McDermott seems to allude to the fact that some of the older parts of the cemetery group the dead by ethnicity, mimicking the Irish, Italian, and German neighborhoods in which they lived, "plac[ing] these New Yorkers in what seems an incongruous kind of order, as if, at their point, order mattered" (*BD* 185). At one point, as Elizabeth and Tupper Daniels are walking on a path beside the East River, and Tupper contemplates how "each one of those lights out there could be a person who lives in New York." Elizabeth replies, "'That's Queens,' . . . but he doesn't hear the contradiction" (*BD* 112). A Queens person would not see Queens as New York, exactly, at least not in the way that Tupper means it. Gazing *from* Manhattan causes Tupper, a newcomer to the city, to rhapsodize about a borough that even its own inhabitants see as inferior. Queens' anomalous state as being neither here nor there, part of New York City politically and geographically but not psychologically, yet not really part of suburban Nassau either, also explains the distinction made by Hedda, the Hamptons innkeeper, who talks about how her daughter was successful in finding her long-lost father, "Right here on Long Island. Well, actually in Bayside" (*BD* 229). To Hedda, Bayside, in Queens, is not actually "here" if "here" means the Hamptons—quintessential, upscale Long Island.

Elizabeth and Tupper's trip to the Hamptons is also described in accurate local detail. Any driver on the Queensborough Bridge from Manhattan to Queens will note the bridge's "steel girders and, on the other side, the shadow of the el blocking from moment to moment what light there is" (*BD* 217). On the Queens side of the bridge, the lanes of the bridge merge with the streets under the "el," the elevated line of the subway, which darkens an otherwise sunny day. McDermott's precise sense of place is not, however, that of her protagonist.

Elizabeth should know the area better than she does since she grew up in a town featuring "shaded avenues named for flowers that is her home" (*BD* 189)—perhaps Floral Park, an example of local geographical schizophrenia in that a Nassau town of that name borders a Queens neighborhood of the same name. No matter in which of the two neighborhoods Elizabeth grew up, she is remarkably ignorant about Long Island roads: "the Expressway, Grand Central Parkway, Southern State, Meadowbrook, Northern State, Cross Island—meet and fuse in her mind, becoming, for her, one long stretch of featureless concrete" (*BD* 182–3). This geographical confusion might suggest the emotional turmoil of her feelings about Tupper because the roads themselves are main arteries, not minor side streets. Long Island, as its name indicates, is a long, narrow stretch of land, shaped roughly like a fish, with its head facing west toward Manhattan and its fins, the North and South Forks, facing east, the Hamptons being on the South Fork in Suffolk County. The east–west roads are the Long Island Expressway; the Grand Central Parkway, the latter changing its name to the Northern State Parkway at the Nassau border; and the Southern State Parkway. These are clearly distinguishable from the north–south roads, the Meadowbrook and the Cross Island Parkways, neither of which leads to the Hamptons.

Elizabeth's unease about traveling on Long Island may mirror the discomfort she feels at leaving Queens, so suitable to her background. She grew up "in a middle-class neighborhood where achievement often implied exile, lonely worldliness and who-the-hell-does-she-think-she-is?" (*BD* 91). This mindset dampens any ambitions that Elizabeth might have developed, making it likely that she will apply for a job as an editor at Vista rather than beginning a career as a writer, or even as an editor in a legitimate publishing house. People from the old neighborhood, no literary sophisticates, are impressed with her title at Vista because they don't understand the difference between a vanity press and other sorts of presses. This is oddly reassuring to her. She takes comfort in her lack of achievement: "Her job was not what it seemed; therefore, despite appearances, she was still herself, still normal" (*BD* 91), Elizabeth's definition of "normal" being unthreatening to those among whom she grew up. For Elizabeth, then, Queens is a state of mind, not just an address. Moving away from it in any sense of the term is uncomfortable on many levels, not least of which is related to the Catholic faith in which she was raised.

Catholicism permeates all of Alice McDermott's novels, and *A Bigamist's Daughter* introduces the people, the places, the material objects, the traditions, the sexual morality, and the theology that make up American Catholic culture, all of which are developed further in her later work. The characters, for example, include a nun wearing a "worn, married-to-God wedding band" (*BD* 25), and the attractive seminarian brother of Elizabeth's girlfriend. Such characters recur in her later novels, as, for example, the nuns in *At Weddings and Wakes* and *The Ninth Hour,* and the conflicted seminarian, then priest, then ex-priest in *Someone.* The schools of the Rockville Centre diocese (which includes Nassau and Suffolk Counties, split off from the Brooklyn Diocese in 1957 as the Catholic population of Long Island increased) are, as they were for McDermott herself, the backdrop for Elizabeth's childhood. The objects associated with the Catholic faith that Catholics term sacramentals are believed to have meaning beyond themselves as physical reminders of spiritual realities. Elizabeth's mother's religious transformation when she moves from Long Island to Maine is indicated by the lack of sacramentals in her new home: "no crucifix above the bed, no rosary beads on the night table, no prayer book, no holy cards, not even the statue of St. Jude, patron of hopeless cases and her favorite apostle, perched on the wide windowsill" (*BD* 27). The absence of these items is an indicator to Elizabeth of how far her mother has journeyed not only geographically but spiritually from her former incarnation as a devout Long Island Catholic.

Elizabeth's unease at her mother's lapses is all the more ironic in that she herself is not conventionally devout. The sexual prohibitions of Catholicism that typically loom large for a single Catholic girl do not seem to have much impact on Elizabeth's behavior. This is obvious when, without giving the matter much thought, she strips for the poet Conrad Sikes; when she engages in casual sexual relationships before meeting Tupper; and when she begins her affair with Tupper himself. Ambivalent, she abandons the strict sexual morality of her Catholicism, but not its vocabulary. She defines herself as an "apostate" (*BD* 111), one who has left the faith, not one who has never belonged to the faith. Nevertheless, when she and Tupper have a discussion of the possibility of an afterlife, she claims to believe in a "typical Baltimore catechism" version of eternity (*BD* 79). The Baltimore Catechism, a compendium of orthodox beliefs in question-and-answer form memorized by Catholic children, is a monument to religious certainty. Originally issued in 1885, the catechism assures its readers that there is, indeed, a heaven, a "state of everlasting life in which we see God face to face, are made like unto Him in glory, and enjoy eternal happiness."[4] This, then, is what Elizabeth believes, even in her self-proclaimed state of apostasy; this is the tribe of which she is a member. When Tupper is disrespectful of her background, telling Catholic jokes that would be acceptable as in-jokes if he were Catholic too, Elizabeth takes offense. Similarly, she resents his dismissal of her Irish heritage as "a misfortune we needn't mention. . . . I was under the impression you'd left all that mackerel-snatching stuff behind you" (*BD* 111). Tupper's contemptuous phrase—"mackerel-snatching"—suggests that his objections to Irish ancestry and Catholicism are based on their lower-class associations.

Elizabeth, the Baltimore Catechism Catholic, retains a belief in the immortality of the individual soul and feels sorry for Tupper, who hopes to achieve immortality via his writing; to him, literary mortality is "the only thing worth achieving: The certain knowledge that when I die, all does not die with me" (*BD* 231). His ambition makes his association with a vanity press all the more quixotic, even given his elaborate marketing plan. Elizabeth feels that Tupper's belief in a literary afterlife is a vain one compared to her own semilapsed Catholicism. Her emotional connection to Catholicism remains and is reinforced when her mother dies. Despite Elizabeth's mother's having abandoned some of the trappings of Catholicism, her funeral includes traditional Catholic elements, and it is these to that Elizabeth responds. When the congregants say the Rosary at her mother's funeral, Elizabeth experiences a longing for the consolation that religious ritual offers: "I wanted it all back. The eternal mother, the immortal confidence. The same prayers repeated . . . the clean taste of a communion wafer on an empty stomach, repeated each Sunday for the rest of my life" (*BD* 126). Repetition is the essence of ritual, and "wanting it all back," the essence of hope.

Vanity of Vanities: On Being a Writer

Derived from the Latin *vanitas,* the term "vanity" has a specific meaning within the Christian belief system: the relative unimportance, even futility, of all worldly things compared to the eternal verities of faith. The common secular meaning of the term "vain" means prideful, and that too has traditional theological implications, pride being the worst of the seven deadly sins. Both meanings of the term operate in this novel. The clients of the vanity press are prideful in thinking that their consuming interest (Mr. Palmer's delusional numbering system, for example) is valuable and worth preserving, if only briefly, in print. But anyone who submits a manuscript for publication does so with the (perhaps erroneous) assumption that it is worthwhile; no books would be published without this act of authorial vanity.

Humility is the traditional antidote to pride, and McDermott seems to possess that virtue in abundance. Her amused modesty is rooted in Catholic culture. In an exchange between McDermott and the author and funeral director Thomas Lynch, Lynch comments that, to Catholics like himself and McDermott, "we are all one and the same children of a loving God," and so none of our achievements "make us anything particularly special," and McDermott agrees, reinforcing Lynch's point by referring to a characteristic Irish expression, "'who do you think you are.'"[5] This is a sentiment she also attributes to Elizabeth in *A Bigamist's Daughter.* Humble though she is, McDermott's early success at finding a publisher for *A Bigamist's Daughter* saved her from the fate of the authors who submit their work to a press such as Vista. The vanity press, that last refuge of the otherwise unpublishable manuscript, is dedicated to "making the dreams of every would-be writer come true, for a while. And then sending them the bill" (*BD* 6).

The novel clarifies how this mendacious enterprise operates. Elizabeth, an editor by title but not by function, does no editing; she is a salesperson, hired "without any experience and only a college minor in English" (*BD* 13). Following her boss' instructions, she learns that the job does not require her to read much if any of the books she accepts for the press. She bases the cost to the author on the page count, to which she adds her estimate of the client's ability to pay; and, as she gets a ten percent commission for any contract over five thousand dollars, she looks for excuses to increase the price. She seals the publishing deal with flattery, comparing her clients' work to that of the giants of literature (this being the only way she can use her college English minor in this job). Vista makes its profit when a contract is signed and payment received. "After that, every penny that is put into production, or advertising, indeed, every book that's sold (for if they sell out the first small binding, they must dig into their pockets to pay for the second), chips away at that profit" (*BD* 281). Vista has no incentive to encourage sales; quite the contrary. The books are sent out for review, but all come back "unopened and unread" (*BD* 152). As novelist Anne Tyler says in her review, "Dusty first editions, some with cruel, tongue-in-cheek jacket covers craftily designed to reflect the art director's disdain, are stacked in the storeroom unsold."[6] Vista only has to make books available for two years, after which cancellation letters go out to the authors. Elizabeth becomes adept enough at this juncture to negotiate a new contract with these same authors on the heels of their previous failure. Elizabeth can only justify her role in this heartless system by imagining herself as a literary St. Jude, "mistress of hopeless cases, of eternal optimists. Mourning and weeping in their valley of tears" (*BD* 286). That last phrase, taken from a Catholic prayer to the Virgin Mary that will be crucial to her later novel *After This,* expresses the Catholic belief that this world is at best a vanity, at worst a place of suffering and lamentation, with Vista Press doing its share to increase the misery.

What is Elizabeth's moral responsibility, if any? The matter is morally ambiguous. Elizabeth can only justify her role at Vista to herself by reflecting that there is a certain amount of callousness involved in every job, and to some extent this is true. If the promised service is provided, what fault is it of the press that authors make too great an emotional investment in the project or expect more than is contained within the four corners of the contract? Isn't it up to the authors to do their own due diligence before they sign a contract with Vista or any other business? If Vista's clients are searching for a kind of redemption in their lives, if they have "dreams of immortality" (*BD* 11), if they cannot even distinguish a sales pitch from editorial guidance, the fault is theirs. *Caveat emptor.*

The novel's exposition of the inner workings of this industry provide is set as a background to Tupper's mission: "To be the first best seller of a house that's known as a joke, to make publishing history" (*BD* 233). He thinks he has a special insight into the psyches of women, the prime readership for fiction, and perhaps he does because he is able to elicit the helpmate instinct in Elizabeth. He persuades Elizabeth the salesperson that she is in fact the real editor she would like to be, one who can contribute valuable advice. It is never clear whether Tupper genuinely loves Elizabeth, but it is clear that what he needs from her is her story, as she is the genuine article, a bigamist's daughter.

Creative Writing 101: The Elements of Fiction

This novel, more than McDermott's later novels, is allusive, full of references to prominent writers, especially those with whom an English minor such as Elizabeth would be familiar: Mark Twain, William Faulkner, Flannery O'Connor,

F. Scott Fitzgerald, Tennessee Williams, Homer. Elizabeth also refers to popular novels of the time, Erich Segal's *Love Story* (1970) and James Dickey's *Deliverance* (1970). Given all her reading, Elizabeth might have noticed, as Anne Tyler does, that the draft of Tupper's unfinished novel has "distinct possibilities."[7] But Elizabeth is not an experienced editor, as was Jonathan Galassi, who immediately saw that Alice McDermott's manuscript was publishable. Against the background of McDermott's later career, the inexperience of her character Elizabeth is the more noticeable. McDermott would eventually teach creative writing at Johns Hopkins University and work with the writing of others much as she depicts Elizabeth working with Tupper on his novel, but McDermott was an award-winning novelist by that point. In lectures and interviews and presumably in her writing classes, McDermott has commented many times on the writer's craft, and this topic is explored in the dialogue between Elizabeth and Tupper. These conversations address key issues with which a would-be writer must grapple, issues about which Elizabeth has only vague ideas.

Tupper's biggest problem, his lack of an ending for his novel, is based on his erroneous belief that a biographical connection is necessary in fiction. Because the living prototype of his bigamist, Beale, is still alive, Tupper has no idea how Beale's life—and, in turn, that of the character based on him—will end. But McDermott would later comment that "what writers want is the *aura* of autobiography," not real autobiography, but "a sense that you know these characters so well you must know them in your own life."[8] When Elizabeth suggests that he should invent an ending, Tupper is surprised but unconvinced, still determined to mine Elizabeth's life for his own use. If in doing so he harms her, he justifies this on the basis that "a good writer sells out everybody he knows, sooner or later" (*BD* 82), principles of common human decency apparently not applying, in his view, to those who consider themselves "good" writers.

Then Tupper has a problem with organization. Elizabeth begins by advocating for the most obvious conventional structure, chronological: "don't you usually tell the past in the beginning? . . . Not at the end?" (*BD* 109). A common analytical tool for students of fiction, Freytag's pyramid, devised by a nineteenth-century German playwright, describes the organization of a plot thus: an introductory situation is represented by a horizontal line; an inciting incident or complication triggers increased tension, represented by an ascending line; a climax, the apex of the pyramid, is the turning point of the action; and this is followed by a sloping line downward, leading to a new state of affairs, represented by another horizontal line, in the conclusion. This is the sort of plot structure that Elizabeth seems to have in mind, the kind of organization a college minor in English would probably have learned in an introductory course. Elizabeth also considers reversing the typical plot structure, suggesting that perhaps Tupper could "end with the past" (*BD* 109). Years later, when McDermott discusses plot structure in her teaching, she uses a different metaphor. She tells her writing students that, once they have "sufficiently described the steady state of their fictional settings and its inhabitants," they should "imagine what [they] have written thus far as a still pond—that's background, steady state. Now throw a rock in it—that's story."[9] Thereafter, to McDermott, it is not necessary that story be told thereafter in chronological order, and McDermott would seldom do so. But whether Tupper thinks of a plot as a pyramid or as ripples in a pool, he still has his original problem: the lack of an ending.

Tupper seems to regard an ending as something that can be tacked on once everything else is written, but McDermott would come to describe a novel's ending as developing organically from the start and indistinguishable from the creation of characters. As McDermott describes her process of creation, the moment of creating her characters leads inexorably to the conclusion of the novel:

> When you start a piece of fiction, in that first line, you can say anything. You are God in his heaven. You are creating the world anew. But once you've written that first line, the second has to follow. And what you've said in the first two limits what you can say in the third. So, forty pages into a story, you don't have every option. You have to be true to the story and the characters as you've created them. . . . Options begin to shut down as you develop a situation and a character. It comes to a point where, as a writer, you feel as if you're not the one making choices for the characters. There's inevitability. The character must do this based on what has come before.[10]

Tupper has clearly not developed this sense of inevitability, of organic development by which the characters have in effect determined their own fates. Thus, he seeks an external source and a real-life precedent to pull together the loose ends of his already-written narrative. The deaths of living people do not necessarily develop organically from their characters or from the way they lived as the deaths of literary characters must, so Tupper's search for an ending in the biography of a living person may be futile.

Narrative voice is another issue for Tupper, and an important one for McDermott. Voice, narration, and characterization are distinct concepts but work together in any fiction. The narrator is the person telling the story; voice is the sense of the narrator as a distinct character. Consistency of narrative voice is achieved in several ways. Once a narrator is chosen, the writer is restricted to the psyche of that narrator. The narrator must, for example, only express what such a person as he or she is might have known or thought. The narrative voice confines the author not just in terms of the information that may be conveyed by that narrator but also in terms of vocabulary and sentence structure. If the narrator is, say, a sixteen-year-old, he or she may only say or think what a teenager might believably say or think. A highly educated narrator can have allowed a large and sophisticated vocabulary; a poorly educated one, the opposite.

Regarding the concept of narrative voice, Tupper has an interesting premise: the story is told in various voices, "various townspeople's theories of who and what he has elsewhere, told from the point of view of the women themselves. So the novel is actually many stories with the same mysterious man as the center of each" (*BD* 12). The townspeople, the "we," are the collective first-person narrators. This is not a technique new to Tupper, however; William Faulkner used it in his 1930 novel *As I Lay Dying,* in which Addie Bundren's family members and Addie herself reflect on her life. Faulkner could create this chorus of voices, but it would be a difficult feat for a first-time writer like Tupper to bring off.

Theme or central concept emerges from the synergy of all the elements of fiction; theme may be a single overarching idea or a multifaceted set of ideas operating on different but related levels. But Tupper seems to think of theme as an add-on, like the moral at the end of a fable by Aesop, rather than implied in the novel's every word. Tupper's formulation of his theme is at once grandiose and commonplace: "I want this book to show that values are meaningless in themselves . . . fragile as glass and useless as dust. I want it to show that value depends only on how you look at things, there are no absolutes. One man's meat, the eye of the beholder. . . . Morality is point of view" (*BD* 144). Tupper thinks these insights are remarkable, but the two clichés ("one man's meat . . . the eye of the beholder") are a clue that Tupper's ideas are actually commonplace.

The idea of shifting viewpoints, however, is crucial. *A Bigamist's Daughter* itself features two types of narrative viewpoints, as some chapters are told by a third-person limited narrator with Elizabeth as the central consciousness, and some chapters are told by Elizabeth herself as first-person narrator. The technical device of shifting viewpoints mirrors Elizabeth's own life. Her story has been shaped by that of her father, and his story differs depending on who is telling the tale. All oral narrative is a complex transaction between teller and listener in which objectivity is impacted by the nature of the storytelling situation. The storyteller may want to present himself or herself in the best light, may want to characterize the opponent in the worst light. Details may be omitted or deliberately concealed. The story itself can be modified by the listener, who, by questioning in the tale-telling moment or remembering later, alters the story, however subtly. The listener then becomes part of the narrative process. At one point Elizabeth asks herself, with regard to her parents' story as told by her mother, "what part of my own memory I would bring to the story as she told it" (*BD* 84). When she tells her father's story (insofar as she knows it) to Tupper, she exercises her own creativity in how she shapes her memories and expands on the partial information she has about her father. In the very process of making this story her own, has she changed it, "imagined [it] herself" (*BD* 195)? Within the oral storytelling tradition, memory and imagination act together in synergy. The complex nature of the storytelling tradition returns as a key element of *At Weddings and Wakes.*

Similarly important for understanding the narrative technique in McDermott's later novels is the role of significant omission. Elizabeth knows that pieces of her parents' story have been left out because her mother "had been raised to believe that to ask any personal questions was to pry," and "she had passed that belief on to" her daughter (*BD* 28). This learned incuriosity results in unanswered questions, mostly about the men in her life: Was her father working for the government? Was he a gigolo, as he claimed to be? Does Tupper love her, or is he using her to finish his novel? Has she really recovered from the loss of her ex-lover Bill? Is anything what it seems to be?

Double Lives: Varieties of Bigamy

Throughout the novel, Elizabeth frequently reassures herself that her work at Vista does not involve deception. Her defense of the industry is that "vanity publishers perform a service and make no promises they don't keep. It's all in the contract. If they seem to promise more than they actually deliver, well, what company doesn't?" (*BD* 103). The emotional involvement of authors in their work is not—legally—the responsibility of the publisher, nor is it the publisher's responsibility to cause the Vista authors to understand what is not included in the publishing agreement. But the fact that Elizabeth feels the need to defend Vista's policies means that she senses a certain duplicity inherent in a job in which she is called an editor but is actually a salesperson. Nevertheless, she persists, and despite her ethical qualms she continues to play both roles.

The double identity that Elizabeth senses in herself is echoed in the pairing of characters in the novel. The most obvious of these is Elizabeth's father, the bigamist, who may have another, duplicate, life and family, and the roots of this doubling may lie in his own early childhood. As Tupper and Elizabeth collaborate on their reconstruction of her father's early life by piecing together a few facts and far more fiction, they arrive at a plausible explanation for her father's (literal and figurative) duplicity. They imagine that, while Elizabeth's father appeared to be the not-particularly-beloved son of a large and impoverished family, he actually was the illegitimate child of the woman he believed to be his aunt. That woman—who may have been Irish pretending to be English, may have been a Bridget disguised as a Betty—has two men in her life, one her child's father, the other her husband, the latter of whom facilitates her reunion with her child, Elizabeth's father. Upon arriving in New York, as Elizabeth and Tupper continue their tale, Elizabeth's father sells his identity to another young man, thus creating yet another double with his same name and his borrowed history. Bigamy provides him with another opportunity to lead a double life.

To reinforce this theme, more sets of pairs appear throughout McDermott's novel. Tupper's fictional bigamist, Beale, has a real-life parallel, Bailey. As a young girl whose father has died, Elizabeth is mistaken for a young girl whose mother has died. Elizabeth's mother, Dolores, has a new lover, Ward; yet on her deathbed, she calls out the bigamist's name. Hedda, the innkeeper, is a serial divorcee but would prefer to be a bigamist. Characters ambivalent about their relationships are connected in odd forms of pairing: for example, Ann, Elizabeth's coworker, is obsessed with, therefore still bound to, her ex-husband, Brian, and Joanne, her girlhood friend, is married to an ordinary man, life with whom bears no comparison to the thrill of her wedding. Via maudlin humor, Margaret Alice Greer's poems of her double mastectomies ("Empty Cups" [*BD* 150] being the most obvious) stress, albeit by its absence, duplication. Tupper himself may be duplicitous, in that Elizabeth is never sure if he is in love with her or just using her to find an end to his novel in her father's story.

For his own creative purposes, Tupper urges Elizabeth to tell him the story of her ex-lover, Bill. Elizabeth, in a solitary farce of a ceremony, had "made *herself* his wife" (*BD* 252; italics McDermott's), seeing in her love for him a hope for the permanence missing in her childhood. Yet she still feared that Bill's loyalty was divided, that he still loved his ex-girlfriend Sarah, and indeed he does return to Sarah after his and Elizabeth's breakup. Even the story of the breakup is highly ambiguous, as Elizabeth tells it to Tupper with several possible endings, one of which is that Elizabeth leaves Bill. Which story is the truth? Elizabeth and Tupper, Elizabeth and Bill, Bill and Sarah: these intersecting couples reinforce the theme of doubling/duplicity. Bill is a shadowy presence impeding her love for Tupper, just as Sarah shadows Elizabeth's love for Bill. Elizabeth eventually duplicates her father's life, leaving Tupper as she (says she might have) left Bill, undertaking the same kind of journey (a business trip) that provided cover for her father's infidelities. As the novel ends, Elizabeth clearly has unfinished emotional business. Just as Bill never lost his love for Sarah, Elizabeth has never been ready to replace Bill. Her relationship with Tupper makes her a sort of bigamist herself. But the real problem lies with her father, not with either Bill or Tupper. Her father's actions have caused her to conflate love with abandonment. So preemptively she leaves Tupper rather than being reduced to the little girl she remembers so clearly, vainly pursuing an evanescent man.

Elizabeth Connolly is a functionary at the lowest level of the publishing industry, but she could be a writer. It is clear that the development of her father's story in Elizabeth's mind shows that it is she, not Tupper, who should claim this creative material for herself. This novel draws from the period in Alice McDermott's life before she took the step away from being something like Elizabeth and toward being a writer. It also documents the emotional risks involved. A young author might well fear that her work would not be seen not as artistry but as vanity. In her succeeding novels, Alice McDermott does not return to the writer's life as a subject but develops further other key elements introduced in this novel: the nature of memory, the function of storytelling, and, most important for her next novel, the geography of Long Island. In *That Night* she demonstrates her abilities as a local colorist of 1950s suburbia.

CHAPTER 3

That Night (1987)

The plot of *That Night* is based on McDermott's memory of an incident from her childhood in Elmont, Long Island. Years later, as an adult, McDermott discussed the incident with her mother, and "learned that the facts of the real story are completely different. When my mother found out what the book was about, she said, 'Oh no, that's not what happened at all.'"[1] The "facts" of this story depend on who is remembering, McDermott or her mother—one a child at the time, the other an adult, but each filtering the incident through her unique perceptions. The ambiguity of memory becomes part of the narrative structure of the novel, and this technique is even more fully developed in *At Weddings and Wakes* and *Charming Billy*. The voice in *That Night* is that of an adult storyteller remembering one summer night in the 1960s when her "ten-year-old heart was stopped by the beauty" (*TN* 3) of an incident involving two teenagers in love. McDermott has given considerable thought to the potential for tragic love in the lives of the young; her essay "Teen-Age Films: Love, Death and the Prom," published the same year as *That Night,* criticizes filmmakers for trivializing the adolescent experience, a fault of which she herself is certainly not guilty. Later she was to explore the psychology of adolescence in *Child of My Heart* (2002) and in the short story "I Am Awake" (2009). In *That Night*, the high drama of a teen romance plays out against the discordant background of a nameless and tedious suburban town.

Some of the critical issues in the novel involve whether the banality of suburbia, and of the lovers themselves, undercuts the tragedy of their thwarted love; whether the doomed attempt of the two teenagers to wring a grand passion out of a bland ordinariness is an instance of heroic failure; and what there is in the narrator's life that causes this incident to reverberate into her adulthood. In terms of McDermott's body of work, this novel establishes her as a local colorist of middle-class family life in suburbia in the 1960s. Her descriptions of physical space, both interior and exterior, constitute a sociological study of the suburban way of life. At the same time, McDermott develops a key theme that would be crucial to her later work: immortality.

Reading Suburban Space

Although McDermott has said that she intended the setting of *That Night* to be "a generic suburb," most critics have compared it to Long Island because of its centrality to her later novels.[2] *That Night* traces the history of suburbs like those on Long Island after World War II, "bedroom communities, incubators" (*TN* 156), that developed rapidly in tandem with a heightened focus on marriage and children. After the upheaval of the war, the physical organization of the suburbs, "the neat pattern of the streets, the fenced and leveled yards, the stop signs and traffic lights and soothing repetition of similar homes all helped to convey a sense of order and security and snug predictability" (*TN* 156). Beneath the surface order, however, is the threat of disintegration. New suburbanites perceived themselves as having not just moved but "fled" from their former homes in Brooklyn and Queens because "the neighborhood—and here they shook their heads, defeated, resigned—had changed" (*TN* 156). They cast themselves in the role of exiles driven forth from ancestral homelands, survivors from a vanished but storied past: "We had parents who spoke to us and each other of the city streets where they had spent their childhoods as lost forever, wiped from the face of the earth by change; who said of their old neighborhoods, 'You can't go there anymore'" (*TN* 157). Catherine Jurca describes this mindset as "a fantasy of victimization that reinvents white flight as the persecution of those who flee."[3] Once Irish emigrants were perceived as lowering the character of a neighborhood, but by the time that *That Night* is set, McDermott's "Irish-American characters feel supplanted or jostled aside by other ethnic groups in New York City, especially nonwhites and/or non-native speakers of English."[4]

This situation recurs in *Charming Billy, At Weddings and Wakes,* and *After This.* Those who flee pity those who stay and try to persuade the holdouts to flee as well. In *That Night, At Weddings and Wakes,* and *Someone,* adult suburbanites try to get their parents to move, but the older generation "remained in embattled city apartments or dilapidated houses buzzed by highways like flood victims clinging to chimneys and roofs, caught by the quick and devastating course of change" (*TN* 157). Change comes to suburbs too. Suburbia is built on shifting sands, threatened by time and circumstance, and every suburbanite is like "those stubborn and curious people who build and rebuild their homes on fault lines" (*TN* 157). For a while, though, the suburban dream seemed achievable, and the postwar era in particular saw the growth of many suburbs like the one in which *That Night* is set.

One such generic suburb is Levittown, in Nassau County on Long Island.[5] William J. Levitt's building of his inexpensive homes coincided with several postwar social trends. After World War II, the pent-up demand for low-cost housing, coupled with the financial incentive offered to returning veterans by the GI Bill and low-interest mortgages for returning veterans, led to a mass exodus of first-time home buyers from cities to suburbs. Between 1947 and 1951, Levitt sold 17,500 houses, immortalizing his name and his vision of suburbia via what McDermott calls the "bland and history-less tract homes" purchased by people like her own parents, "who in previous and more interesting lives had been born in the city, raised in the city, educated, romanced, employed in the city"; and, of course, there was "no need to specify which city, there was always only one."[6] In reality, suburban life had its charms, but in fiction, "suburbia has never had a very good rep. . . . That man-made purgatory of our modern culture, situated at some precarious point halfway between the city with its violent grittiness and the small town with its long-kept secrets and fresh-bread smells, the suburb, for all its popular idealization, is usually frowned upon in the halls of high culture."[7] With her second novel, McDermott examines one such suburb and its population of exiles from the semi-urban world of New York City's outer boroughs.

These new suburbanites were more likely to identify as residents of the Long Island towns in which they now lived than with the ethnic parishes of Brooklyn and Queens from which they came. Catholicism, so important in all of McDermott's other novels, plays a much smaller role than social class in *That Night*. The towns and the neighborhoods within them rise and fall in prestige depending on the housing stock. Dramatic differences in housing prices across Long Island mean that even the names of neighborhoods within these towns become signifiers of social class. Even a nondescript suburban town like the one depicted in *That Night* represents a step up—but only one step, not a giant leap—from the urban boroughs. Social class markers are in the details, and all of them indicate that this is a lower-middle-class neighborhood.

The sights and sounds of the suburban neighborhood are more obvious in the summer, when its residents are more likely to be outdoors and to have their windows open, thus hearing and seeing each other's cars, the ice cream truck, lawn sprinklers, lawn mowers, window fans in those days before air conditioning became a commonplace, garbage cans hauled to the curb, "the collective gurgle of filters in backyard pools" (*TN* 4). Those gurgling filters hint at another class marker: the sound can be heard, so the lot sizes are small, and the pools are probably the small above-ground type, cheaper and inferior in quality to in-ground pools. Small building lots also mean that residents can hear each other's "arguments . . . strained, echoey exchanges between husbands and wives, parents and children" (*TN* 11), and observe each other's comings and goings. All these details indicate that these houses are on the lower end of the local price range.

Clothing and behavioral details signal social class as well. One resident is "sitting on his front steps with a beer" (*TN* 12), a reminder of the sociable summer evening stoop gatherings of Brooklyn and Queens but uncommon in higher-end suburbs, where the residents are more likely to use private outdoor spaces. Some of the men on the steps are in "white T-shirts and gray suit pants," indicating that they have jobs which require them to wear suits but also have no qualms about appearing in public without the dress shirts that go with those pants. One Mrs. Sayles is "the only woman in our neighborhood to wear tennis whites to the supermarket," these items of clothing, and the sport itself, signifying upper-class leisure and trendy athleticism; but her outfit is incongruous with that of her husband, who "wore gray work clothes and carried a lunchpail" (*TN* 12). Mrs. Sayles has either married down or is aping the customs of her social superiors, or both.

Details of individual houses are indicative of the people who live in them. Sheryl's house, for example, shows signs of neglect since her father died, suggesting that a traditional division of labor across gender lines has left her widowed mother incapable of maintaining the exterior of a house. The hedge, in a most visible spot, is bedraggled. In a more affluent neighborhood, handymen and landscapers would take care of these maintenance chores. Any such sign of neglect is magnified by the contrast with the other houses on the block, all alike but better maintained. In an attempt to individuate these cookie-cutter examples of midcentury mass-produced homebuilding, some families have painted the front steps red or white or a combination of both. But since the painting becomes a neighborhood trend, Sheryl's house is individuated by default since the steps remain the "plain dull brick-color bricks" (*TN* 9) installed by the developer.

Inside, in the women's domain, the details of Sheryl's house presage Sheryl's mother's response to her daughter's pregnancy. The living room seemed "soft and comfortable," suggesting that Sheryl's mother has some capacity for warmth. But the fact that her decorating choices are aesthetically uninspired ("velvet paintings . . . plastic slipcovers" [*TN* 56]) indicates a tendency to mindless conformity. Plastic slipcovers are an attempt to preserve furniture, sacrificing appearance and comfort for the sake of economy; affluent people would more likely use the couch in its uncovered and more comfortable state. The slipcovers make the couch feel as if "sheathed in a thin layer of ice" (*TN* 56), forecasting Sheryl's mother's reaction to the pregnancy: sterile and cold.

Another implied critique of suburbia is exemplified by the Carpenters, a set of suburban grotesques who live in their own basement. Ironically named in that they have built nothing but purchased everything, the Carpenters are shown by their house to be consumers, not craftspeople. The house references all the insecurities of the social class that populates this typical suburban town. They have earned the money to buy all the items in the house but behave as if they are unworthy of actually using them. The narrator momentarily sees Mrs. Carpenter as "more artist than eccentric" (*TN* 96), but that interpretation is undercut by the relentless banality of the basement decor, with its

> wall-to-wall carpeting and pine paneling and a television built right into the wall . . . a kitchenette, a dining table, a bath with a stall shower . . . curtains on the tiny windows and crushed-velvet throw pillows on the sofa and the chairs, and these had been bought specifically for the basement, not merely demoted there after long and faithful service in the living room. There was the requisite bar with padded swirling stools and a ceramic drunk holding onto a lamppost (*TN* 92).

Since all their actual activities are accommodated in the basement, it seems normal to them that they spend all their time there instead of in a house "too beautiful to bear" (*TN* 93). Chairs are too precious to sit in; bedrooms must be vacated upon arising. As if it were a museum, the house is exhibited by Mrs. Carpenter to admiring housewives like the narrator's mother. Curator of kitsch, Mrs. Carpenter has reduced her own status to that of caretaker, tour guide, and guard.

Outside the houses, suburban spaces are gender- and age-specific. The women are tied to their houses by housework and child care; the only one of the mothers who leaves the neighborhood is Rick's, and her destination is a mental hospital. In the days of the one-car, one-driver family, the women's range of motion is limited to the neighborhood, public transportation being sparse in suburbia. Within it, however, and during the day on weekdays, they range freely through the "kitchens and dining rooms and side doors" of their neighbors (*TN* 17). The men, on the other hand, leave every weekday to work but when home are housebound themselves, living on the perimeters of their little patch of real estate, "puttering on the lawn or taking the garbage to the curb or sitting on their porches" (*TN* 17). The novel attributes this male behavior specifically to the effects of World War II. Their modest properties represent peace and security to them after the horrors of war. All this changes the night Rick, a rebel with a cause, comes for Sheryl. This triggers a confrontation between the suburban dads and the "hoods" (*TN* 6). The "respectable fathers" revert to military type, banding together, sensing a "new expansion of their territory, the recalled camaraderie of men joined in battle" (*TN* 24), this time to protect their home turf.

On an ordinary day, those same streets are the habitat of children, who, accepting no boundaries, "roamed through our neighborhood like confident landlords . . . strolled easily over any lawn, hopped into any yard, crossed driveways and straddled fences" (*TN* 17). The teenagers, too young to own private space but wanting it anyway, are mostly depicted in the outdoor spaces that they have claimed as their own: the mall, schoolyards, bowling alleys, "parking lots and movie theaters and public playgrounds" (*TN* 113). Rick and Sheryl use public outdoor space as private space when a park's most secluded area, away from the roads on which police cruisers patrol, becomes their bedroom.

The inevitable pregnancy leads her mother to send Sheryl into what the girl perceives as exile, to Ohio, to the Wayside School, its very name conjuring up the fallen woman stereotype. Homes for unmarried mothers of the time period seemed to have been predicated on the notion that teens who get pregnant need to be incarcerated, that "girls in trouble" are ipso facto "troubled girls" (*TN* 83). Not yet known as single parents, "unwed mothers . . . fell somewhere between criminals and patients and, like criminals and patients, they were prescribed an exact and fortifying treatment: They were made to disappear" (*TN* 85–86). Sheryl's escape from the house in Ohio and her failed attempt to get home is an effort to restore her life to its pre-pregnancy state.

One of the novel's major ironies is that, were she not imprisoned herself by conventional ideas about unmarried mothers, Sheryl's mother could find a meaning and purpose in the care of Sheryl and her child. Adrift in a world of couples after the sudden and premature death of her husband but unimaginative enough to accept without question the received wisdom that in such situations "the girl must disappear and the hoodlum boy never know" (*TN* 53), she unwittingly exacerbates her own grief. Even the children, in their efforts to figure out the facts of human reproduction from the partial information offered to them, realize that "a child as marvelous as any one of us would be born" (*TN* 109) of Sheryl's pregnancy. In her incomprehension of that fact, Sheryl's mother shows herself to be part of a larger social malaise, a mindless conformity.

Love, Loss, and Immortality in the Generic Suburb

Belief in the immortality of the soul in *That Night* is a response to grief and loss. Damaged by the death of her father, Sheryl compensates by devising her own theology of the afterlife. The central tenet of her own personal faith is that her love for Rick is related to her love for her father and that both are evidence of the immortality of the soul. Love like this, she believes, cannot come to nothing, cannot be wasted, must continue beyond death. If such love fades, hope for an afterlife dies also. The theological dimension of the novel is intimately connected with the narrative viewpoint. The narrator, too, has suffered a loss, and her intense interest in the story of Sheryl and Rick is a function of her own unresolved grief for her aborted fetus and her hope that this loss too will somehow be made right.

Several of McDermott's novels employ unconventional narrative viewpoints, and this is true of *That Night*. Some of the novel is based on the narrator's direct experience: as a ten-year-old, she witnessed the event of "that night"; she heard what others in the neighborhood said about these events; and she had one highly significant conversation with Sheryl. The rest of the novel constitutes the narrator's reconstruction as an adult of the love story of Rick and Sheryl. The narrator's imaginative embellishing of the tale is obvious, in that the narrator describes scenes at which she could not believably have been present: Sheryl's telling her mother that she is pregnant, Sheryl's trip to Ohio, and Sheryl's suicide attempt in the diner bathroom. But the narrator was present at the most important conversation, which occurs when the narrator is ten years old. In it, Sheryl explains how she sees the relationship between her love of her father and her love for Rick as evidence for the immortality of the soul. For Sheryl, love is a "demonstration that the dead are not gone."[8]

Unlike the narrator, the adults around the couple do not understand the transcendent significance of Sheryl's love for Rick, so they trivialize the relationship and assume it is temporary. Pam, Sheryl's cousin, tells Sheryl the story of her own failed teen romance: "I met someone else. I got over it" (*TN* 137). Pam cannot know that Sheryl's love for Rick gives her hope for reunion with her father: "the girl had linked her father and Rick, the way she had determined to love them. She couldn't have known that for Sheryl, bereft as she was, peace was annihilation and to say that love could fade, that loss could heal, was to admit forever that there would be no return of the dead" (*TN* 138). To "get over" Rick is to lose her father all over again, and forever.

"Even children know you cannot separate the tale from the teller" (*TN* 157): this insight applies to all McDermott's narrators. In *That Night* the narrator's absorption in Sheryl's story must be related to her own life, and in particular to the narrator's abortion. At the time, the narrator believed the abortion was right and necessary to preserve her fledgling relationship, but her marriage failed anyway. Father and child moments—Pam's husband's holding his child in a way that Rick and Sheryl's child will never know, a gesture echoed when, years later, Rick embraces his own child—are associated in the narrator's mind with her own lost child and accounts for her emotional involvement with Sheryl's loss of her father. The narrator remembers and takes some comfort in Sheryl's "strange assurance" that loss "would not be forever. It wasn't possible that two people who loved each other could be apart forever" (*TN* 89). Sheryl does not understand that her love for Rick is a function of her unresolved grief for her father; even the adult narrator, older though she is and wiser though she should be, perceives only dimly the relationship of her own loss of her unborn child to her preoccupation with Sheryl and Rick's story.

Years later, the narrator learns that Sheryl has married and had other children. And Rick, too, reappears, accompanied by his wife and children, to see the house of the narrator's parents, which is up for sale. The narrator notices that his adult persona, of which his appearance is only one element, bears no resemblance to that of the doomed but heroic young man who came to claim his beloved that night. From the physical description it appears that Rick has prematurely settled into early middle age and bored domesticity. His casual, perhaps dismissive comment on his relationship with Sheryl—"I dated her in high school" (*TN* 163)—seems to suggest that he has gotten over Sheryl, but in context, with his wife and children waiting in the car outside, talking to a stranger on his way through a house for sale, it would be hardly believable for him to discuss his lost love. How does the older Rick feel about Sheryl? Did he know about the baby? The matter is left unresolved.

That Night is the only one of Alice McDermott's novels to be made into a film as of this writing,[9] and as films adapted from novels do, it offers its own interpretation of the narrative. The film is a social/psychological study of a girl's coming of age via involvement in a problematic teen pregnancy narrated in voice-over by a ten-year-old Alice. She and her prepubescent neighborhood friends are absorbed in discovering the mysteries of sex and childbearing, and Sheryl and Rick provide them with a case study. This is especially true for Alice, whose voyeuristic interest in watching Sheryl (their bedroom windows are directly across from each other) is at once a sex-ed research project and an escape from her parents' bickering. Rick and Sheryl are a stereotypical greaser-boy-and-Catholic-schoolgirl pair, but portrayed sympathetically, especially Rick. Before the pregnancy, he seems sincerely devoted to Sheryl and is especially insightful and sensitive regarding Sheryl's loss of her father. Once he realizes that Sheryl is pregnant, he pursues her, intending to marry her and raise the child.

Some scenes in the film strain credulity, such as when, in order to sustain the fiction that Alice is witness to key events, she tags along on a steamy all-night date with the two lovers, and when, without her parents' knowledge, she goes with Rick on his journey to rescue Sheryl from the unwed mothers' home.

Some important elements of the novel are changed: the sympathetic Ohio relatives who take pregnant Sheryl in are deleted and replaced by a facsimile of the novel's Wayside School, a prison-like home for unwed mothers run by a stereotypically strict Catholic nun; the diner where Sheryl stops to eat becomes the site of the couple's reunion. The film ends with a hint of the facile happily-ever-after characteristic of so many film adaptations, offering a gleam of hope that Rick and Sheryl can in fact rise to the occasion, join forces, and keep their baby, all in the face of bourgeois disapproval.

In the character of Sheryl, the novel reaches for a far higher meaning than the film does. Confused and immature though her thinking is, Sheryl believes that human love is nothing less than evidence for the immortality of the soul, that such love cannot be destroyed by death, that memory truly, not just metaphorically, keeps the dead among the living. These otherwise undistinguished suburbanites—Sheryl, Rick, the narrator herself—are grappling with an age-old spiritual longing. On that night, the night Rick came for Sheryl, eternal love seemed possible.

McDermott's third novel, *At Wedding and Wakes,* reprises the themes of setting and memory that form such a large part of *That Night.* In this novel, local color is bound up with the larger theme of Irish emigration to America. Historically, the Irish emigrant typically did as these characters do: they arrived in New York and settled in the outer boroughs. That emigrant generation connects the family to its roots mainly via the memories of Ireland conveyed through storytelling. The second generation, the audience for these stories, coexists in an uneasy tension with the Irish past, and this tension is expressed in the geography of Long Island.

CHAPTER 4

At Weddings and Wakes (1991)

At the heart of Alice McDermott's *At Weddings and Wakes* is a Brooklyn apartment, the family home of four women: Mary Towne ("Momma") and three of her four stepdaughters: May, Agnes, and Veronica. The fourth stepdaughter, Lucy, has married and moved to the Island, Nassau County, but, except for two weeks in which she and her family vacation even farther east in Suffolk County, Lucy returns to Brooklyn twice a week throughout the summer. On these pilgrimages Lucy is accompanied by her three children, who hear Momma's stories of the family's past in Ireland and America and from whose collective viewpoint the events of the plot are narrated. More than any of her other novels to date, this novel is firmly set against the backdrop of Irish history, especially the emigration experience.

In interviews McDermott has been known for "sedulously disclaiming any intention to be the laureate" of Irish American Catholics.[1] She has said that she doesn't "really feel that the Irish American experience is . . . [her] subject,"[2] that she has "no inherent interest in Irish Catholic families in New York as such."[3] Instead, she claims to have arrived at the subject as if by default since it is what she knows, her "material at hand"[4]: "I know Irish-American people. I know what their homes look like. I know what they have for dinner. I know how they turn a phrase."[5] In *At Weddings and Wakes,* this knowledge manifests itself in details of setting and characterization but mainly through narratives of the family's past in Ireland and America, transmitted to the young by the sole surviving member of the emigrant generation.

The Storytelling Tradition

McDermott's novels rarely connect her characters' stories to events in the larger world, but *At Weddings and Wakes* is an exception. In Momma's apartment in Brooklyn is a copy of a *Life* magazine commemorative issue, published on December 14, 1963, "that featured on its cover a formal portrait of President Kennedy edged in black and inside . . . a full-page photograph of Mrs. Kennedy in her black veil" (*AWAW* 19–20). The present-time action of the novel takes place during the summer of 1964, the summer following the assassination of John F. Kennedy. But to the Towne women, life in the present is less significant than life in the past, stories of which are told whenever they gather: stories of the shipboard romance of the four sisters' emigrant parents Annie and Jack Towne in 1913 or 1914; of the emigration of Annie's sister Mary seven years later to help Annie, then expecting her fourth child; of Annie's death following Veronica's birth; of Mary's marriage to Annie's widower Jack; of Jack's death. As the three Dailey children, Bobby, Margaret, and Maryann, travel by bus and subway to their mother's family home in Brooklyn, they journey also into the family's history. They are watching as their mother, Lucy, is torn between two opposing views of the world: that of Momma, her stepmother Mary, and that of her husband, Bob. Momma embodies the collective memory of the Irish emigrant experience—and memory, says McDermott, is a "story-building process."[6] Bob, on the other hand, represents the next stage of the Irish American experience, the world of middle-class suburbia, into which he attempts to draw his family. Lucy's painful conflict is embodied not only in significant people, her stepmother and her husband, but also in the novel's key settings, Brooklyn and the Island.

In Brooklyn the children hear the stories of their family. Storytelling in this novel operates within the context of a long tradition. According to Kathleen Vejvoda and Clodagh Brennan Harvey, traditional Irish stories can be categorized by content: they might be tales of the great heroes of Ireland's past, both historical and mythological; they might be folkloric tales of supernatural beings; or they might be family sagas.[7] Family narratives are traditionally the province of women; accordingly, Momma is "the woman storyteller refashioning the tales of her tribe."[8] Refashioning means that when a tale is told several times, some details are added, some are omitted; there is no one accurate version but rather a series of reshaped narratives. The stories told at Momma's are shaped by the presence of the Dailey children. Although the stories are, and are meant to be, in a repeated phrase, "part of everything they knew" (*AWAW* 145), concealment and incomprehension are built into the whole situation. Subjects must be avoided, obvious questions must be unanswered, oblique hints must substitute for definite statements, partly because the answers might be painful but also because the Dailey children are present.

The location of this family's storytelling is also congruent with the tradition. As McDermott notes, many American families act out "that sense of paying homage" to the past via "the journey back to grandma's place . . . those long afternoons of visiting relatives."[9] In *At Weddings and Wakes,* the twice-a-week trips to Brooklyn when Lucy and the children hear these family tales are a New York variant on the Irish tradition of storytelling "*ar cuirt,*" "on a visit."[10] Summer afternoons provide the time and Momma's Brooklyn apartment the venue. At such gatherings in Ireland, it was common for tales to be modified to fit the audience—as, for example, "an audience of women and children"[11]—and so it is in Brooklyn. Having the gathering at Momma's apartment, not at Lucy's suburban home, is in itself a significant statement. In Ireland, it was customary for tales to be told only in certain houses, the *ceili* houses,[12] and only by the *shanachie*, the official storyteller. Momma's storytelling asserts the primacy of the Brooklyn apartment and of Momma herself.

As the emigrant, Momma is the sole arbiter of Irish authenticity. Her view of the mother country, however, is unremittingly negative. Although Momma left as a young woman and thus might be expected to see Ireland through the haze of childhood memory, she is relentlessly antinostalgic. She and her sister Annie left Ireland primarily for a personal reason, to escape their stepfather, "the drunk in the parlor" (*AWAW* 137), in Jack's mocking expression, rather than the political and economic problems that drove so many others away. Yet Momma is contemptuous of all things Irish, even the songs played at May's wedding. The three songs, imitations of emigrant ballads ("Galway Bay," "My Wild Irish Rose," and "I'll Take You Home Again, Kathleen") echo the ballads' sense of loss and longing for Erin. The Irish American wedding guests are awash in sentiment for a land they never visited and never would, especially if they had to endure hardship as their forebears did: "not one of them would have gone home again—across the ocean wild and wide—for anything" (*AWAW* 195). In historical fact, first-generation Irish emigrants returned to Ireland in far fewer numbers than members of other emigrant groups; as William Shannon says, going home for them "would be a journey back in more than one sense . . . into the womb of old memories and long forgotten sadnesses."[13]

At least one of these sadnesses, Ireland's political turmoil, is suggested in the verbal confusion, in a discussion of John F. Kennedy, between the name of Charles Stewart Parnell and the innocuous term "parallel." This leads to someone exclaiming, "Sweet Jesus, don't mention Parnell" (*AWAW* 195). The allusion is to the argument over politics at the Christmas dinner in James Joyce's *Portrait of the Artist as a Young Man.* Parnell, a charismatic political leader whose career was destroyed when in 1889 his long-term liaison with a married woman was revealed, remains a controversial figure because of the role played by the Irish clergy in driving him from public office and, some believed, to his death two years later. In Brooklyn or Queens, as in Dublin or Belfast, political discussion can ruin a social occasion. It is acceptable to speak of Kennedy in 1964, still fresh in people's memories as the apex of Irish American Catholic success, but the story of Parnell is one that should not be told.

Momma does want the children to remember (her version of) the key stories of the family's life: emigration, birth, marriage, death. First among these in historical order are the emigration stories of Annie, Jack, and Mary herself. Annie and Jack leave Ireland separately in 1913 and Mary in 1920. With the death of her mother, Annie had no secure place at home and no protection from her drunken stepfather. On the ship, Annie meets Jack Towne. While May idealizes this "shipboard romance" (*AWAW* 68), the marriage can also be seen as a practical one. Marrying Jack enables Annie to achieve two common goals of post-famine Irish women emigrants: to marry and to secure "an independent adult status."[14] Marrying Annie protects Jack from loneliness and guarantees him a home and family in his adopted country. Each serves the other as a link to their shared Irish past.

Annie's marriage places her in a position to do what was customary among Irish women in America: to become a link in the emigrant "chain," one emigrant facilitating the passage of another,[15] and her sister Mary arrives in 1920. Mary's emigration story is told in the form of a recognizable tale type, that of the greenhorn in the big city who spends all her money in the ship's chocolate shop and thus arrives penniless. Mary has come to family members, which saves her from the consequences of this rookie mistake. Because her mother is dead and there are no further links in the family chain to be brought over, Mary does not need to send money home. So it is that she can work in her sister's household without pay, and so it is that she is free to marry Jack after Annie dies.

Fred, who will marry May, tells his own mother's emigration story, which both parallels and amplifies that of Mary Towne. His telling it establishes his own historical connection with their shared Irish past. Fred's mother's life follows another common pattern in the life of Irish emigrant women: domestic service as the first—and, for her, the only—job in America. From the post-famine years onward, as Hasia R. Diner points out, Irish women considered domestic service more desirable than factory or mill work, and due to increasing prosperity, demand for household help became so heavy that it outweighed prejudice against the Irish and placed servants in a favorable position.[16]

As Maureen Murphy points out, "Irish girls who found work in the smaller households were often treated as members of the family, albeit as children."[17] Even with this condescension factored in, domestic service had advantages for Irish women. Compared to Irish men, who were commonly employed in dangerous, unhealthy industries like construction and mining,[18] Irish women fared better as domestics. The kind treatment that Fred's mother receives illustrates this point. They allow their housekeeper not only to live out but to care for her own child while on their payroll. The excellent location of the family's home on Central Park West enables Fred's mother to send him to school in Manhattan. Fred's mother's story demonstrates the resiliency of Irish women emigrants, and this becomes part of what the Dailey children, two of them girls, come to know.

The Banshee in Brooklyn

Tales of the supernatural, like that of the mysterious man in the stained-glass window, are also part of the storytelling tradition. Of all the family's stories, none is more powerfully connected with the Irish past than Momma's tale of hearing the cry of the banshee outside the window of the apartment building in Brooklyn. The story is told in three separate versions, each adding some details and dropping others in a way characteristic of oral narrative.

The first, briefest version of the story suggests, but does not state, that the sound is that of the banshee: "Momma, standing beside her dying sister, had turned (part of everything they knew) when from the sudden, menacing stillness there arose an awful, lovely, distant cry that had made her scalp bristle" (*AWAW* 84). The second version is more detailed and more specifically situated within the banshee tradition: "More than forty years ago she had stood above her sleeping sister, who was feverish but not yet dangerously so, still exhausted, they'd assumed, by a difficult birth, and had seen the light grow flat and felt the air become hollow and had heard the distant but unmistakable cry of what no one in the family, retelling the story, would call a banshee, knowing how foolish it would sound" (*AWAW* 86). Both of these versions of the experience are consistent with the Irish folklore tradition.

Patricia Lysaght, an authority on the banshee, defines it as "a female spirit said to presage death in certain families."[19] Momma's repeated retellings of the story contain elements that are consistent with the folklore tradition and authenticate the experience. The banshee's most characteristic feature is the sound she makes, her "cry."[20] The sound is described as utterly unique; in one account from County Waterford in the 1930s, the uniqueness of the sound lies in its "loneliness" and "some other element of strangeness in it"; another account, from County Sligo, described the cry as "weird."[21] The sudden stillness that Mary senses at her sister's deathbed is also mentioned as accompanying the banshee's cry in a tale collected in County Cork in the 1970s: "Suddenly there was dead silence and this awful *caoin* ['lament'] started."[22]

Telling the story to Veronica, Momma alters the story slightly. She describes the physical manifestations (the change in the light, the sudden stillness) that have been part of her story before but adds another, the motion of the curtains on a windless summer day:

> She said: "I stood by her bed, you know, just after you were born. It was hot, hotter than Hades. Your father had taken the girls for a stroll, toward the river, he'd said, where they might catch a breeze. You were in the cradle in the other room. I stood by the bed. She was feverish, but who wasn't in that heat. In a day or two, I figured, she'd be back to herself. And then the light just flattened out, like the life had gone out of it. I looked out the window. The world had never been so quiet. And then I began to hear one sound. I saw the curtain move, although I can tell you there was no breeze. I turned back to Annie. I stood right next to her. She was thirty-eight years old and she had three children and a new baby and a husband, and I had waited seven years to be with her. You and your sisters can talk about your newspaper tragedies, your camps and refugees, but for me this was no less than any of it. For me this was the worst thing. When Mrs. Power came up she scolded me for shutting the window, the old biddy, but all I cared about by then was that she get the doctor." (*AWAW* 89–90)

Unnatural wind manifestations, according to banshee lore, can predict or announce a death.[23] Mrs. Power's scolding of the young Mary for closing the window is a detail added to the story in this retelling. Mrs. Power's reaction establishes that the window was closed when she arrived, and Mary testifies that "there was no breeze," yet the curtains moved. This manifestation indicates the presence of the death messenger.

The fact that Mary and only Mary hears the sound is also consistent with the tradition. It is common for the cry to be "clearly heard by some people but inaudible to others."[24] Only those who will live can hear the banshee because the cry is a signal to the community to prepare for its impending loss. Mary's hearing the banshee, ironically, marks her off as a survivor. While a cry is mentioned at the sudden death of Jack Towne, Momma makes no claim that it was also the banshee. She hears "a cry of sorrow like she'd never heard, and by the time they reached him he was gone" (*AWAW* 64). If Momma had never heard such a cry of sorrow, this is not the cry of the banshee, which she has in fact heard before.

For various reasons, according to Lysaght, belief in the banshee in Ireland, much less in America, has undergone "substantial weakening."[25] This accounts for the ambiguity with which the banshee's cry at the deathbed of Annie is described: "the distant but unmistakable cry of what *no one in the family, retelling the story, would call a banshee,* knowing how foolish it would sound" (*AWAW* 86; my italics). If by the 1920s such belief is diminishing in Ireland, the idea of the banshee crying outside an apartment window in Brooklyn would seem even more foolish. But some elements of the banshee tradition do support the possibility of a banshee in Brooklyn.

Crucial to banshee lore is the idea that only certain families are "followed" or "cried" by the banshee.[26] The banshee is associated not only with certain families but with certain places. The banshee's cry is usually heard "at or near the house in which the person was dying";[27] the banshee was thought to be spiritually connected to the ancestral homestead in Ireland. But when an entire family has emigrated, banshee manifestations in the United States and Canada have been reported.[28] So Mary's (ambiguously expressed) claim to have heard the banshee outside the apartment window is consistent with both her role as conduit of the family's Irish heritage and her efforts to make the Brooklyn apartment into an American equivalent of an Irish family homestead.

The deterioration of this family's belief in the banshee is seen, appropriately, in a humorous comment by that representative of the Irish American future, Bob Dailey. When May dies, the suddenness of her death, like that of her father, precludes anyone's hearing the banshee's cry. Even if May's death were not sudden, the banshee would cry at the family home, not at a rented vacation cottage. While the banshee does not cry for May, the tradition is echoed in Bob Dailey's description of his daughters' playful shrieks on a summer night: "'Oh, hush,' he called to them. 'You sound like a couple of banshees'" (*AWAW* 206). Bob's skeptical comment is followed by another, more natural, presaging sound: Mrs. Smiley's knocking at the door.

Geography and the Tribe

Momma Towne's phone call, interrupting Lucy's Long Island vacation as she had done so many times before, is a reminder of Momma's function in the family as a human version of the death messenger. Bob Dailey sees Momma as the dead hand of the past, the antithesis of all the suburban contentment he desires for his family. But on the other hand, she is also the one who has kept the memory of the dead alive. This self-assigned role requires that she reassemble her family to mourn their dead, which can only be done at the family home, the Brooklyn apartment.

The significance of the apartment as the locus of the family's experience in America is explained in detail by Claire Crabtree-Sinnett. Annie Towne died in a makeshift bedroom created by partitioning off part of the living room with a curtain; Mary Towne will not sleep with her new husband "until the 'shanty Irish' curtain . . . was replaced by a wall" for additional privacy. Within that wall, Agnes has hidden Annie's journal, and this "buried book," Crabtree-Sinnett says citing McDermott herself, "represents secrets in families."

Veronica's "exotically decorated back bedroom" is the scene of her problem drinking. Even the apartment's liminal spaces are significant:

> the window seat where the children can watch for dramas in the street outside or their father's long-awaited headlights: the fire escape where May, her feelings hurt by ridicule of her romance with Fred, spends an evening unnoticed: and the entry and stairway where . . . the masculine footsteps of their father Bob or Fred can be heard approaching. But the spaces that might mediate between the tragic past and the open future are themselves potentially dangerous, like the landing where Jack collapsed and died.[29]

If the apartment is a safe space, the world outside is unsafe.

Long Island, however, is familiar turf for the Irish—indeed, is a microcosm of the history of the Irish in the New York area. When the Irish emigrated to New York, they tended to remain within the five boroughs, if not in Manhattan itself, then in Brooklyn and Queens just across the bridges. As Hasia R. Diner points out, there were good reasons for this: "For one thing, it took money to venture far beyond the port of arrival, and to leave New York, Boston, or Philadelphia to farm required more capital than most Irish had with them. Also, Irish newcomers harbored negative sentiments about the agricultural life. Since they had left Ireland precisely because of the limited—or, more accurately, shrinking—opportunities of farm life, they showed no eagerness for it in the United States."[30] While Momma is inaccurate in imagining Nassau County in the 1960s as rural, she is typical of her generation in her preference for an urban environment. Apartment life provided a familiar quasi-communal living arrangement. According to Peter Quinn, the New York apartment building provided a simulacrum of "the traditional Irish village, or *clachan* . . . a clump of cabins that leaned on one another, a physical embodiment of the tight-knit community."[31] Momma is typical in her reluctance to move. Even for the next generation, moving is difficult: when Fred, May's fiancé, wants to change his life after the death of his mother, his idea of change is moving to another apartment within the same building.

In Brooklyn Momma recreates a semblance of the Irish homestead in a city apartment. It is in the apartment that the four Towne sisters were conceived and born; there that Annie died, the banshee crying at the window; there, in the hallway outside the apartment, that Jack died. The apartment is a place of refuge for the damaged Veronica and the place to which those who flee (May, Lucy, their half-brother John) must return, albeit briefly, in the case of John. Elements of Irish life are recreated within the apartment. The unmarried daughters—the "old girls"—live there. The ubiquitous lace curtains, a sign of "the arrival of the Irish into the realm of the middle class,"[32] shield the windows. Other Brooklyn/Queens details authentic to the period signal their lower-middle-class status: the women's hairnets, their aprons, the clotheslines upon which they hang laundry from the apartment windows. Their sense of place is indicated in a Catholic way, by the name of their local parish. Brooklyn is home and so seems safe to them. To Lucy, life in Nassau County seems a form of exile in comparison to life in Brooklyn; when Lucy and her family leave at the end of a visit, they are provided with a shopping bag of provisions, as if embarking on a dangerous journey to an unknown land. This gesture is echoed in *Charming Billy* by that of Dennis Lynch's mother, who packs food for Dennis and Billy to sustain them on their journey from Queens to what she sees as the uncharted wilds of eastern Long Island.

Because of the centrality of the apartment to the family's life, Momma measures the safety of her stepdaughters by their proximity to it. For any of them to leave Brooklyn, even for short trips, is threatening to her. This is especially true of Lucy's living in Nassau and venturing further, either to the North or South Forks, for an annual vacation. Several critical analyses of the novel have noted that the family's movements in space from west to east are manifestations of Bob Dailey's "attempts to evade Towne history" by leaving, if only briefly, "purgatorial Brooklyn" with its "constriction and enmeshment" in the past.[33] Momma finds any excuse to reverse this outward motion, to pull Lucy back. Phone calls announce at least a problem, often a death, requiring the gathering of the clan. Momma could easily withhold the information of minor mishaps or deaths of nonfamily members until the Daileys' vacation is over, but that would be to fail in her role as assembler of mourners.

Lucy and Bob's move to Nassau County also places them in a slightly higher social class than their Brooklyn family. Crossing geographic boundaries, as in *A Bigamist's Daughter* and *That Night,* has social, economic, and psychological dimensions. Crossing the city line represents another chapter in the emigrant story. Second-generation Irish Americans like Lucy and Bob Dailey are "certified Irish Americans, their children born in America."[34] People like them often moved to Nassau County, and to them this move meant progress. According to Margaret O'Brien Steinfels, a "side benefit" of the move would be "extracting the second-generation parents from the strictures of immigrant households, like Momma Towne's, which hold them captive to the family sorrows and disappointments."[35] This typical benefit obviously does not accrue to the Dailey family because Lucy is a willing captive, but many who moved to the suburbs did so to live differently from their parents. To those parents back in the urban boroughs, their adult children's move meant rejection of their upbringing. Momma is not entirely wrong about this. She has failed to keep her son, John, nearby, so she attempts to keep her stepdaughters close to home (three of them remain *at* home). While Irish "family bonds stretched across the ocean,"[36] Momma fears that, because of social class and lifestyle changes associated with the move, such bonds will not stretch from Brooklyn to (adjacent) Nassau County.

Suburban life in all of Suffolk and most of Nassau was then and remains now mainly dependent upon the automobile. In 1964 Lucy Dailey does not drive. Since Lucy takes public transportation (an intricate series of buses and subways) from her home to Momma's twice a week, it is clear that the Daileys must live in one of the parts of southwestern Nassau County that has public transportation links to Brooklyn. Fred took public transportation to and from his home in Woodside, in Queens, when he has his first mail route in suburbia. When Fred and May consider buying a house themselves, Bob suggests towns in southwestern Nassau and even Queens: Garden City, Valley Stream, Bellerose, Rosedale, Floral Park, which straddles Queens and Nassau. These towns are linked to the subways that serve Brooklyn by that umbilical cord of Long Island transportation, the Long Island Railroad. Bob's suggesting such towns is not just about simplifying Fred's commute to his postal route; Bob is implicitly warning Fred that the Towne women cannot separate from their birth family, from the old neighborhood, from their Momma, from the past.

If the pull of the old neighborhood was so strong, why did the second-generation Irish Americans move at all? What were they looking for in Nassau that they could not find in Brooklyn? Fred calls it "another kind of life" (*AWAW* 121). The images that Fred uses to describe suburbia—growth, change, the birth and education of children, shiny new material comforts—embody the hope that suburbia offered. But Momma wants no changes, even for the better, in the lives of her stepdaughters. She has the emigrant generation's fear, having already traveled far, of traveling farther. To her, suburbia's trees and grass remind her not of burgeoning new life but of rural poverty.

> "Grass and flowers and trees," she said. "Sounds like a cemetery to me. . . . No one has to tell me about the country," she said. "I was born out in the country"—did they know that? And they nodded, yes, yes, it was part of everything they knew. A farm, she said, and now her hands were raised to shield her from the memory. An awful place, she said, but smiling, nearly laughing, as if at the foolishness of anyone who would think otherwise. Just awful. (*AWAW* 145)

To Momma, suburban life on Long Island is equivalent to rural life in Ireland, so she seeks any excuse to discourage May's move. The lure of home ownership, which drew so many to Nassau and Suffolk, is to her just a way of squandering money.

When Fred and May discuss their plan to buy a house, Momma disapproves of what she sees as the financial risk and scoffs at the notion that the whole family might share in the newlyweds' suburban dream. Momma's evidence of Fred's improvidence is the diminishing cost of the bouquets that he brings to May over the course of a month, suggesting to her that he is unable to manage his salary so that it lasts through the month. If Momma is right, then Fred, otherwise with his secure civil service job a good candidate for home ownership, may indeed have trouble paying a mortgage. But Momma is wrong in equating the value of Long Island real estate with drooping daisies: a modestly priced Long Island house purchased in 1964, when Fred and May were engaged, would have typically increased in value fivefold over the ensuing twenty years. What Momma fears is not Fred's alleged improvidence but the loss of May.

In this fear she is more realistic, having the example before her of her son, John. In John's case, a move to suburbia has either been caused by, or caused, a loosening of family ties. John lives in Staten Island. Unlike Nassau and Suffolk Counties, Staten Island really is an island separate from Brooklyn. Before 1964, when the Verrazano-Narrows Bridge was opened, travel between Brooklyn and Staten Island was by ferry from lower Manhattan only. From 1964 on, the present-time action of the novel, efficient car travel from Staten Island directly to Brooklyn was inaugurated. This would imply that John could visit his mother and half sisters more often. But by then John has insulated himself from his birth family, visiting for only an hour a year on Christmas day, and he brings up his children to have an even more tangential relationship to family than he does. In contrast with John, Bob Dailey's decision to live in a suburb accessible to Brooklyn by public transportation does respect his wife's family ties more than John does his.

Bob's wife, however, is not satisfied with this compromise. Lucy and Bob Dailey's irreconcilable differences on the matter are expressed in terms of the geography of Long Island: "The journey of their struggle . . . was west to east. She, Lucy, his wife, pulling them in to the thickest, most thickly populated part of the Island, to the swarming city where they'd both been raised; he, when his two weeks opened up before him like a trick door in what had seemed all year to be the solid wall of daily work, taking them out to the farthest, greenest reaches of the Island, to the very tip of the two long fingers that would seem to direct their eyes, as he himself would do each evening, to the wide expanse of the sea" (*AWAW* 38). At the root of Lucy's discontent with suburbia are issues larger than her husband, larger than her stepmother, larger than the rivalry between them for her allegiance. For one thing, Lucy's suburban malaise is particularly relevant to her situation as a member of a diaspora, a scattering of a tribe. As Catherine Jurca notes, the sense of "displacement" that Lucy feels is common among emigrants, and even the children of emigrants. It manifests itself in a sense of "disparity between the place one inhabits and that place somewhere else where one imagines one's real home or homeland to be."[37] As is clear in her affect when she returns to her real home in Brooklyn, she has failed to form "cultural connections"[38] to the suburbs. But Lucy's problem is far deeper than a failure of adjustment to suburban housewifery. Lucy, and only Lucy, must choose between her mother's vision of family as inextricably linked to the Brooklyn apartment, scene of the family's births and deaths, and her husband's vision of a new kind of family life in suburbia.

An even larger issue affecting Lucy involves the relationship of the present to the past, of the living to the dead. Lucy's incessant need for her Momma is not only a case of failure to launch but also a need for "some constant acknowledgment of the lives of the dead" (*AWAW* 205). Lucy has always rationalized her trips to Brooklyn as being altruistic, not for herself but "as much for May as for Momma" (*AWAW* 14) and, after May's death, "to make up for May" (*AWAW* 159). Lucy prefers to think of the Brooklyn family as the object of her charity, but deeper psychological processes are at work. Her journey to Brooklyn on subway and bus is a "journey underground, to the land of the dead,"[39] like the journey Sally makes on the train in *The Ninth Hour.* Hence the increase in the frequency of her trips after May's death.

Momma is a complex character; not merely a harbinger of doom and destroyer of joy, she is also a link with the Irish past. Important values may be lost to upward mobility and mindless homogenization. This is dramatized by the episode at May's wedding when Lucy's daughters meet two older women from the Brooklyn neighborhood. At the wedding, these two, the Miss McGowans, make the usual small talk that adults employ in conversation with children. But then: "One of them pointed at the older girl. 'And there's Annie's face at that age, as clear as if I'm remembering her,' she said. The other nodded. 'Lord, yes, God love her. There she is'" (*AWAW* 182). McDermott stresses the significance of the first woman's comment by repeating it, in italics: *"Annie's face, at that age"* (*AWAW* 183). The Miss McGowans, who knew Annie as a girl, link her American granddaughter to her across time, even across the great divide between life and death. This ritual element, this "dealing with the dead,"[40] may be lost in the generic suburb.

McDermott's next novel, *Charming Billy,* further develops many of the same themes as in *At Weddings and Wakes.* For Billy Lynch, the real world is Bayside, Queens, where he lives with his wife, Maeve; his ideal world is the

Hamptons, where he met his beloved Eva. The storytelling theme is repeated also, in that it is the narrator's task to piece together the different versions of Billy's life told by the various observers of and participants in it. Billy's story, however, cannot be understood apart from the theological concepts of Catholic Christianity.

CHAPTER 5

Charming Billy (1998)

In her 2003 essay "The Lunatic in the Pew: Confessions of a Natural-Born Catholic," Alice McDermott notes ironically that "while developing into a mediocre Catholic I have also, simultaneously it seems, become a Catholic novelist." Some discussion of McDermott's novels focuses on her place within the Catholic literary tradition and on the extent to which her fiction reflects her personal faith.[1] The topic addressed here is how Catholicism functions in the world of McDermott's fiction. In her (thus far) best-known and Pulitzer Prize–winning novel *Charming Billy,* "Irish Catholic Queens New York" (*CB* 32) is an all-pervasive environment, providing a setting, a group of stock characters, a symbol system, a complex web of assumptions and customs, a language, and a code of ethics, all of which are related to, but sometimes in conflict with, a coherent theology.

Professions of Faith, Admissions of Doubt

McDermott has been specific, detailed, and consistent over a long period of time about her beliefs and her doubts, and three essays in particular are essential reading in this regard. In "Confessions of a Reluctant Catholic" (2000), McDermott describes her upbringing in a Catholic household. Her parents were not strict traditionalists but readily accepted changes in the Church following Vatican II. The three children of the family, including Alice herself, rebelled in high school, deceived parents about Mass attendance, and critiqued the Church on the basis of their nascent intellectualism. McDermott's parents tolerated their children's being religious slackers while still encouraging them to return to the Church. McDermott's brothers never did, but she did: she describes herself as "a practicing Catholic. A reluctant, resigned, occasionally exasperated but nevertheless practicing Catholic with no thought, or hope, of ever being otherwise." She sees her own "religious evolution" not as a "triumph of faith" but rather as an example of how people like herself "finally . . . choose the faith we were given . . . a church we have, at various times in our lives, seen as flawed, irrelevant, outdated, impossible, and impossible to leave behind."[2]

In "The Lunatic in the Pew: Confessions of a Natural-Born Catholic" (2003), this ambivalence is on display. Although claiming to be "not a very good Catholic," McDermott nevertheless writes this moving profession of faith: "Being Catholic is an act of rebellion. A mad, stubborn, outrageous, nonsensical refusal to be comforted by anything less than the glorious impossible of the resurrection of the body and life everlasting." Nevertheless, on her first trip to look at a Catholic school for her child, she has an aversive reaction: "It was all too familiar: the uniforms, the orderly rows of desks, the crucifixes and holy water fonts and carefully colored cutouts of little lambs and big-eyed shepherd children. The Catholic school smell, which most especially brought back the terror and the tyranny of my own Catholic grammar school. . . . I was nearly hyperventilating." Despite these misgivings, she did send her children to Catholic schools, and sends her characters into similar Catholic environments.

By 2013, in "Redeemed from Death? The Faith of a Catholic Novelist," McDermott has come to embrace the designation, which ten years earlier had seemed so ill-fitting, of herself as a "Catholic writer": "What makes me a Catholic writer is that the faith I profess contends that out of love—love—for such troubled, flawed, struggling human beings, the Creator, the First Cause, became flesh so that we, every one of us, would not perish. I am a Catholic writer because this very notion—whether it be made up or divinely revealed, fanciful thinking or breathtaking truth—so astonishes me that I can't help but bring it to every story I tell." Yet she is also critical of the institutional Church. In 2017, in an interview at her alma mater, Sacred Heart Academy in Hempstead, New York, she describes herself as embarrassed by the "grave moral error" of the Church's attitude toward women and by the clergy sex abuse scandal, an embarrassment exacerbated by her role as a "public Catholic." So faith-filled yet so ambivalent, McDermott, who repeatedly describes her personal religious practice in self-deprecating terms, "mediocre," "not . . . very good," and "lackluster yet persistent," has developed into the foremost contemporary American writer in the Catholic tradition.[3]

In the Catholic world that McDermott creates in her fiction, time itself is shaped by rituals: baptism, confession, communion, confirmation, weekly Mass attendance, meatless Fridays. Settings include Catholic schools and Catholic churches. Irish Catholics like McDermott's characters particularly enjoy the social aspects of religious practice, "the after-events of church-going . . . [like] the party after a sacramental moment."[4] The material culture of

Catholicism surrounds them, some objects verging on absurdity ("the big plastic statue of Mary with the glow-in-the-dark rosary beads in its base"[5]), others richly symbolic (lighting candles in church for special intentions). As people of faith but poorly educated in that faith, McDermott's characters often engage in "ridiculous moral and physical acrobatics performed in order to maintain and defy the letter of church law."[6] The right amount of detachment from this insular world is provided by the first-person narrator, Dennis' adult daughter, who has married and moved to Seattle. Through her eyes the reader comes to see how this Catholic world both shelters and confines its inhabitants.

A Parallel Universe: The Catholic World

Catholic types and stereotypes populate McDermott's fiction. Billy Lynch himself is a stereotype, McDermott says; there is "just such a stock character in so many extended Irish-American families."[7] Typical priests perform typical functions, sometimes perfunctorily, as when an unnamed priest says a "quick blessing" (*CB* 3) over the food at Billy's funeral lunch, and sometimes professionally, as when the monsignor consoles the mourners at Maeve's house afterward, "like an expert, a pro, like a slugger going to the plate or a surgeon to the operating table, a renowned attorney rising for his closing arguments . . . someone who knew what he was doing" (*CB* 151). Such men may not be saintly, but they do their jobs, even Father Ryan, himself a whiskey priest, who accompanies the alcoholic Billy on his journey to Ireland to "take the pledge" to quit drinking (*CB* 4). Imagery associated with the Roman Catholic clergy is used to describe Billy and his cousin Dennis: Billy wears glasses "that you once saw only on priests and nuns" (*CB* 52); Billy is "as elegant as a pope" (*CB* 52); Dennis, in conversation with Billy, "listen[s] like a diligent priest" (*CB* 62); and when Dennis asks his stepfather, Holtzman, a shoe store owner known to all only by his last name, for a loan, Dennis "nodded, murmuring like a priest" (*CB* 122). Both young men, raised among clergy, unconsciously echo contrasting clerical types: "The aesthete priest and the jolly chaplain" (*CB* 63).

Imagery associated with Catholic nuns is used to describe Maeve. In her early childhood, the sisters of the local parish serve, willingly and free of charge, as her widowed father's after-school child care. Secure and content in the quiet, orderly convent, Maeve considers joining a religious order herself (a situation that will recur in McDermott's 2017 novel *The Ninth Hour*). Instead, she accepts the traditional role of the "old girl," the only or last child, expected to live at home and to care for her elderly father. Long after Maeve marries Billy, the aura of the convent lingers. Her hair, at Billy's funeral, is "cut short as a nun's" (*CB* 3). Her apparent lack of sexual desirability leads the mourners to see her as a consolation prize for Billy after his loss of Eva, his grand passion, and they even imply that Billy and Maeve's marriage might have been childless because it was celibate. So strong is this connection of Maeve with the convent that right at the funeral luncheon, "Ted Lynch went on about an order of nuns that takes widows" (*CB* 149). This seems the life for which a woman like Maeve is destined; it occurs to no one that she will marry again.

These Catholic types move within and between Catholic settings, inhabiting a parallel universe, the cradle-to-grave institutions that were first established in the United States in the nineteenth century to protect Catholic immigrants from proselytization or discrimination. The New York area Catholic high schools mentioned in the novel (Regis for boys, Mary Louis Academy for girls) feed into the local Catholic commuter colleges (St. John's, Marymount, Malloy [*sic*]), or, for the more venturesome, the out-of-town colleges (Holy Cross, Canisius, Notre Dame); thence, for those interested in post-baccalaureate education, Fordham Law. The Catholic alcoholic need not venture into Alcoholics Anonymous, which Billy calls "a Protestant thing" (*CB* 14), but could "take the pledge," an Irish Catholic thing. Were Billy to go to a doctor, there would be Catholic doctors affiliated with the Catholic health care system; the fact that he dies in a Veterans Administration hospital is a consequence of his having collapsed on the street. When Billy dies, a Catholic funeral director arranges his funeral, and he is buried in what appears to be St. Raymond's Cemetery in the Bronx, just over either the Throgs Neck or the Whitestone Bridge from Bayside, where he and Maeve lived. When widowed Maeve gets a job, it is in a Catholic environment, a "little job Ted Lynch found for her with the archdiocese" (*CB* 241).

This close-knit tribe maintains beliefs about the afterlife that they associate, sometimes erroneously, with their religion. Some of these, like the Celtic pagan concept of the banshee in *At Weddings and Wakes,* are closer to superstition than to the faith of theologically educated Catholics. One of the funeral luncheon attendees is not unhappy about the inclement weather because "rain on a funeral day is supposed to mean a soul going straight to heaven" (*CB* 166). All funerals remind them of Billy Sheehy's father singing "Danny Boy" at Uncle Daniel's gravesite, a song that locates Danny Boy's dead parent as a consciousness below ground, neither perfectly happy in heaven nor suffering in hell but waiting longingly for Danny's return to Ireland. In "Galway Bay," heaven in specifically located in the west of Ireland. Billy's own vision of the afterlife is similar to that expressed in "Galway Bay," as he—only half-jokingly—locates the afterlife with geographic specificity, on Long Island, in Suffolk County, in the Hamptons. None of these beliefs are consistent with Catholicism.

The conversation of the Legion of Mary ladies at Maeve's house after the funeral luncheon further illustrates the influence of folk beliefs. The Legion of

Mary is a traditionalist volunteer service organization operating under Church auspices; its members commit themselves to practicing good works in the community, of which visiting the bereaved is one example. Advanced education or a sophisticated theological mind would not be a necessary requirement for membership. Thus, it is not surprising that the "shorter Legion lady" offers the soothing but improbable observation, which she attributes not to Catholic doctrine but to a vague group of "colored people," that "No one's called home who isn't ready" (*CB* 147).

This same Legion lady also recounts three dreams of her dead husband, dreams that she construes as communications from the afterlife, meant to "put [her] mind at ease" (*CB* 148). Heartened by the thought that the dead can facilitate healing in this manner, the "taller Legion lady" (*CB* 148) and Billy's sister Rosemary cite the number of these dreams as further proof of their veracity, the mystical significance of the number three being a folkloric commonplace. According to Patricia Coughlan, traditional Irish beliefs about "widows seeing their dead husbands—'always three times'—in dreams," is a way of expressing the need "to relinquish the dead,"[8] similar to the way the cry of the banshee prepares for the death in *At Weddings and Wakes.* Such supernatural experiences as these dreams, especially in the days following soon after the death, reflect a corollary belief that the "newly dead are felt not to have yet left their familiar haunts,"[9] which accounts for Maeve's mistaking Dennis, coming in with the dog, for the dead Billy. This "after-event of churchgoing," the gathering at Maeve's house in Bayside after the funeral luncheon, which is itself after the funeral, is as important as the liturgy itself,[10] but it is at this point incorporating pagan rather than Catholic traditions.

A Common Tongue: On Speaking Catholic

The main function of Catholicism in McDermott's writing is, she says, linguistic: "to give my characters a vocabulary that they might not otherwise have. These are people who would not know how to give language to their experience, who would not know how to say, 'There's got to be something more than this' . . . if they couldn't also say 'redemption' or 'ascension.'"[11] Catholic-speak, then, is the characters' "first language."[12] McDermott's writing style is also influenced by "the liturgy, the prayer, the gospels—[which] was in many ways my first poetry,"[13] and "prepared me for literature through chant, repetition, set prayer."[14] But as for abstract doctrinal statements, McDermott says she is "not interested," so concepts like "conversion, transubstantiation, the mystical body of Christ, the infallibility of the pope, Aquinas, or Augustine" do not usually form part of her characters' vocabulary.[15] Billy's "theology of alcoholism," his drunken meditation on Christ's redemptive sacrifice on the cross, is an exception.[16]

Few of her characters—with the exception of some, but not all, of the priests and nuns—have received a serious theological education. The religion of most of the characters is not an intellectual commitment but rather an emotional connection, "genetic, cultural, blood-borne,"[17] and its vocabulary the lingua franca of the tribe. The characters share a common stock of references. Everyone knows what "First Communion shoes" (*CB* 13) look like; everyone bows the head at the mention of Jesus's name; everyone fasts during Lent and before communion and dresses up a bit for church; everyone understands lame Catholic jokes and refers to neighborhoods by the names of their parishes. Bishop Fulton J. Sheen is on the radio, St. Francis presides over birdbaths, rosaries are said, candles lit. McDermott is expert at depicting the details of churchgoing, especially the comical little breaches of ecclesiastical decorum like the sound made when Maeve's father, drunk at her wedding, "banged his foot against the kneeling bench—you could hear it all over the church" (*CB* 16).

Catholic rituals express belief via physical objects and sensory experience. Just as in *A Bigamist's Daughter* Elizabeth Connolly is soothed at her mother's funeral Mass by the sound of familiar prayers, by the feeling of rosary beads in her hand, by the taste of the communion wafer, Billy Lynch is comforted by the sensory elements of his faith: "the good sound of the familiar Latin, the same women every morning saying their beads, the red sanctuary lamp, and the candles beneath the statues of the Virgin and St. Joseph, steadfast and true" (*CB* 111). The unchanging nature of ritual, repeating itself year after year, provides Billy with hope that Eva's love for him will be "steadfast and true" as well. Both Billy and Dennis go to Mass and weddings and baptisms at various churches to fulfill their "need for faith, for that which was steadfast and true" (*CB* 113). The repetition of the phrase "steadfast and true" is itself influenced by the formulaic and repetitive language of prayer.

McDermott occasionally uses the exact words of the liturgy, as, for example, when in an interview she expresses her faith thus: "I look for the resurrection of the dead and the life of the world to come."[18] Catholics in the audience would immediately recognize the phrasing as taken verbatim from Nicene Creed, recited during the Mass. Other expressions in *Charming Billy* are derived from the Common of the Mass, its fixed prayers; the Proper of the Mass, its seasonally changing scriptural passages; the memorized prayers of a Catholic school childhood; the Rosary, a series of rote prayers counted off on a set of beads; and especially the litany, a repetition-with-variation set of invocations to the Divinity, to Jesus's mother, Mary, and to the saints. McDermott uses this ritual language throughout her work. The inclusion of Catholic prayer types in her fiction is a manifestation of her belief that, even in nonreligious contexts, "already-formed words" provide a consolation that ad hoc linguistic formulations do not, serving to compensate at times when "our individual words are insufficient when we are faced with grief and sorrow."[19] The litany in particular accounts for a particular characteristic of McDermott's style: repetition, sometimes with variation, of especially significant phrases. This prayer type will be particularly influential in *After This,* taking center stage in a key passage in that novel.

Catholic language in *Charming Billy* provides the writer with a shorthand method of developing characters. The tribal bond is reinforced by the quick appeals to saints, to the Virgin Mary, and to Jesus interjected into ordinary conversation, as if no matter is too trivial to call to the attention of spiritual powers. When Uncle Daniel, the importer of emigrants, is called a "Holy Father" (*CB* 39), a veritable pope, almost a saint, everyone knows what that means. They would also catch the reference to Daniel's patronage of immigrants, enabling "one wetback mick after another being reeled in from the other side and slapped down on their couch" (*CB* 39), as associating Daniel with the apostle Peter, "fisher of men."[20] Dennis's mother's life is a "purgatory" (*CB* 103), miserable but temporary, until Uncle Daniel frees her. Billy's trip to Ireland is a "pilgrimage" (*CB* 15), a journey to a holy place. All of these may seem more like verbal tics than affirmations of faith, but McDermott reminds her readers that these characters need this vocabulary to express themselves; they have no other.

What to Believe, How to Behave: Doctrine and Ethics

In addition to a common language and symbol system, the characters share a set of moral norms enforced by a long-since-internalized system of rewards and punishments. Dennis's and Billy's sexual history, for example, is a testimony to the efficacy of Catholic indoctrination. "The Paulist Fathers had gotten them at an early age" (*CB* 70), long before puberty, and initiated them into the Catholic version of the shame and guilt culture. Before they enlisted in the military, Billy and Dennis functioned in a setting so homogeneous that it seemed that all women of their group were off limits. In the military, at the height of their sexual attractiveness, "handsome in their uniforms and perfectly fit" (*CB* 70), fear of death weighed heavily upon them, and to commit serious sin was to risk eternal damnation.

After the war, Dennis's behavior changes, but not his beliefs. Early in his relationship with Mary, she and Dennis have a sexual encounter. Dennis, in keeping with Catholic moral teaching, defines this act as a sin; at the same time, he is rather proud of having "something to tell the priest [in confession] at St. Philomena's on Saturday" (*CB* 85). Thereafter, he vacillates, "taking the subway when he had resolved to sin no more, Holtzman's car when just one more was the current resolution" (*CB* 113). He can joke about guilt with Billy—"Guilt is glorious . . . When it's well earned" (*CB* 90)—but he never questions the underlying concept that he has been taught in childhood: extramarital sex is a sin.

Thoroughly indoctrinated with the tenets of his faith, it never occurs to Dennis that his behavior would be wrong even if he were not a Catholic. For the sake of "a few minutes of animal grunting and bumping," he makes "promises . . . to Mary at moments when the girl had every right to believe him" (*CB* 119). But he does not love Mary and does not intend to marry her unless he has to, which for Catholics of his generation means that if she becomes pregnant, he will do what was thought to be the right thing and marry a woman he does not love. Even if this morally murky situation does not arise, Dennis is wrong in accepting Mary's love under false pretenses. Although the story of their relationship is never told from Mary's viewpoint, it seems that sex, for Mary, involves a more serious commitment to Dennis than his to her. When Eva's betrayal of Billy gives Dennis an excuse, he discards Mary and later reduces her to a comic stereotype, "Irish Mary," and jokes about her to his family. What Dennis has done is wrong not just because the Catholic Church forbids it but because it is inauthentic, deceptive, and exploitive. Since Dennis does not possess a vocabulary of sexual ethics apart from Catholicism, he appears to assume that his eventual "good" confession (which, conveniently, coincides with his waning interest in Mary) also obliterates the harm he has done.

The characters also demonstrate their allegiance to the faith by engaging in debates on issues that are only meaningful within the Catholic community. Clerical celibacy, a discipline not embraced by other Christian denominations, is one of these. Celibacy, Dan Lynch thinks, sets a priest apart from a minister who lives an ordinary life, has "dinner with his wife and kids" (*CB* 171). Dan sees a radical incompatibility between marriage and family life, and what he imagines the Catholic priest's life to be, "lived on another plane . . . A life that's all God, nothing else" (*CB* 171). To Dan, there is something "holy," "special," especially because of sexual abstinence, which involves "sacrifice" (*CB* 171). Dan's thought processes here contain several errors and omissions. He assumes that celibacy is both cause and effect of transformative faith. He cannot imagine that "a wife and a mortgage and new shoes for the kiddies" (*CB* 172) can also provide a path to holiness. Being unmarried, he assumes that there are no sacrifices involved in family life, in paying that mortgage or buying those shoes. Why might Dan Lynch be so enamored of the concept of clerical celibacy? At

Billy's funeral luncheon, Billy's sister quotes her mother as saying, "there's nothing more pathetic than an old bachelor who's not a priest" (*CB* 17). Dan Lynch's stance on the celibacy issue might be an unconscious attempt to justify his own "old boy" lifestyle by associating it with that of the clergy.

As regular churchgoers, the characters share a common stock of knowledge of biblical stories that they apply to their own lives, sometimes to their detriment. Maeve thinks of her life before Billy in terms of the Martha/Mary story in the Bible (*CB* 132), a story with a message that is ambiguous at best. In the Gospel of Luke (10: 38–42), Jesus visits a household consisting of two women, Martha and her sister Mary. Martha serves the dinner while Mary sits at the feet of the Lord, listening intently. Martha, "burdened with much serving," complains about being cast in the domestic role while Mary plays the intellectual role, and Jesus corrects her. Mary, says Jesus, "has chosen the better part" and should not by discouraged from doing so. The biblical story ends then, with Martha put in her place, a place of service. Maeve interprets this story to apply to her own situation as caretaker of her father. Thinking only in terms of the oft-repeated story, Maeve assumes that she has freely "chosen" her dutiful daughter role rather than having been trapped in it by way of paternal expectations, limited options, and her own passivity.

Billy, too, thinks in terms of biblical imagery, and this habit of mind is a factor in his obsession with Eva. Billy was happy with Eva in the Hamptons; therefore, he associates the Hamptons with heaven and with its earthly foretaste, the Garden of Eden in the Book of Genesis. When Billy thinks of Eden, he identifies with Adam, all innocence and trust. He does not, however, take this analogy to its next logical step. If he is Adam, then Eva is Eve, the temptress who loses Paradise not just for Adam but for the whole human race. Eva's husband, in his overalls at his gas station in Clonmel, is a lame stand-in for the serpent in the garden, the Prince of Evil. But the fall is real. Billy, having transformed Eva into a quasi-supernatural figure, is unprepared for the petty flaws of an actual human being and is broken by his discovery that Eva betrayed him long ago, and for so meager a reward. This betrayal is all the more poignant in that he discovers it in Ireland, itself the "lost Eden" of Irish American fantasy.[21]

The characters' shared faith is also a source of gentle humor—the Catholic joke, often the stuff of sermons—as, talking among themselves, they give their most deeply held beliefs a satirical spin. In Catholicism, deathbed conversions are believed to be acceptable to God in reparation for the misdeeds of a lifetime. Dennis's mother's deathbed conversion is an example of this principle: "in a recapitulation that must have left even the heavenly host momentarily voiceless, [she] decided during the closing days of her life to make an end run at heaven" (*CB* 37). The sports metaphor—calling up a ludicrous image of Sheila

Holtzman, abandoning her ironing board once and for all to carry a football past all obstacles through heavenly goalposts—renders her late-stage piety ludicrous. The narrator and her brothers, shifting the metaphor to gaming, see her actions as "not so much as a deathbed conversion but as a final-hour placing of bets, a closing-time rush (as my oldest brother, the philosophy major, put it) to get a piece of the action in Pascal's wager" (*CB* 41). The philosopher Blaise Pascal (1623–1662) posited that it makes more sense to gamble on the existence of God than not to do so because, if there is a God, the payoff is infinite; if there is not, the penalty is nil. So Sheila Holtzman's contributions to the Catholic Church and to charitable organizations are her way of engaging in theological gamesmanship. The language of sports and gambling puts a humorous spin on Sheila's conversion, but also on the belief in last-minute repentance, which has always seemed slightly unfair to the longtime righteous, those who identify with the Prodigal Son's reliable brother.

Similarly satirical is the debate between Dan Lynch and Rosemary about which of Sheila's two deceased husbands will take marital priority in the afterlife. Dan Lynch doubts that Holtzman, a wealthy man at least by Queens standards, would have made it to heaven because Christ warned about the low probability of a rich man's entering the kingdom of heaven, comparing such an event to a camel's passing through the eye of a needle (Mark 10:25). Holtzman's exclusion from eternal bliss would solve this two-husband problem neatly, leaving the field open to Sheila's first husband, Uncle Daniel. Without comment on the worthiness of Holtzman, the taller Legion lady avers, "with an easy expertise," that the rule in the afterlife is this: "The first marriage is the binding one" (*CB* 143). How she achieves such certainty is unclear but kinder than Dan Lynch's consignment of the genial Holtzman to eternal damnation.

Dennis and Claire's vision of marriage in the afterlife involves one comic and one serious dimension. Both operate on the comforting assumption that Claire will be in heaven, a saint, not in the canonical sense of someone approved for veneration and emulation via an official ecclesiastical process but in the sense of being among the saved. She will then be in a position to help her husband, who will depend on her in death as he did in life. So needy will Dennis be that Claire's perfect happiness will be tempered with exasperation at her husband's peskiness, much as a living wife might tire of her husband's repeated requests for domestic assistance. On a more serious note, Dennis's devotion to his wife in her final year, the growth of their relationship in anticipation of its lasting into eternity, is an illustration of just how little Dan Lynch knows about the spirituality of marriage. The words of the wedding ceremony—"till death do us part"—are, for Dennis and Claire, a promise kept, a mission accomplished: "they would love each other until the last moment of her life—hadn't that been the goal from the beginning?" (*CB* 46). Dennis and Claire experience God because of, not in spite of, their marriage.

Ironically Dan Lynch, so wrong about so much, seems to be the only character who experiences unwavering faith. The monsignor who comes to Maeve's house after the funeral teaches the official theology of immortality: death is not final. Billy's "life goes on, in Christ . . . with the hope of rising again" (*CB* 153). McDermott's acknowledgment in her essays of the difficulty of this kind of unwavering faith is expressed by her unnamed narrator here, Dennis and Claire's daughter. She, like Elizabeth Connolly in *A Bigamist's Daughter,* sees herself as an "apostate" (*CB* 51), apostasy being "an act of *refusing to continue to follow,* obey, or recognize a religious faith."[22] The very definition suggests that one cannot be an apostate without having once been a believer. The same ambivalence is contained within the narrator's comment that she and her father "had long ago given up arguing about the niceties of our Church" (*CB* 51). Self-proclaimed apostate though she is, her phrasing suggests a residual connection to Catholicism: it is (still!) "our Church," ours, and with a capital C; and it is only the "niceties," the trivial details, about which they argue, not the essentials. Her father's faith is shaky too, but in a different way. After Claire dies, Dennis has passing thoughts of the "illusion" that is "Church-sanctioned" (*CB* 32) and cannot believe that "heaven was any more than a well-intentioned deception" or that death was "anything other than the void" (*CB* 211). These two, the narrator and her father, are not the Baltimore Catechism Catholics described in *A Bigamist's Daughter* (79); their belief, such as it is, incorporates struggle and doubt.

Difficulties of faith culminate in a key scene in the novel, Billy's drunken attempt to ask what is for him the ultimate question: how, in the face of the utter obliteration of the self that death appears to be, is it possible to believe in an afterlife? How is it possible not to believe? Could God have created human beings so full of potential, only to allow them to die? Is death God's ultimate con, cheating a person of all that their lives may have yet promised, just as Billy believed Eva's death at a young age did to her? Doesn't the theology of Christ's death and resurrection serve as proof that one must rage against death as Billy rages, must never recover from the pain of losing a loved one because that would minimize the horror of death? Billy, poorly educated and drunk, cannot put these thoughts together to form a logical chain of reasoning as a trained theologian could. But the sense of the passage is clear. Two conflicting thoughts must be held in the mind at the same time: the Catholic faith professes a belief in eternal life; that belief is hard to maintain in the face of the terror and insult of death.

As the novel ends, the question remains: Does the difference between what is "actual," what is "imagined," and what is "believed" make "any difference at all" (*CB* 243)? Perhaps the most faith-affirming image in the novel draws on the Catholic doctrine of the community of saints, the unbroken relationship between the living and the dead. This concept provides a counterweight to Billy's refusal to stop mourning the loss of Eva. Billy has missed the theological point: the doctrine of the communion of saints means that the dead are not lost, are still united with the living. The poet, essayist, and funeral director Thomas Lynch, in a discussion with Alice McDermott, says that "the notion of closure is probably one of the great stupidities that we foist on one another. It is not the way it works."[23] The "way it works" is illustrated in the final scene of the novel.

Poet and essayist Dana Gioia writes that the Catholic faith is "intrinsically communal . . . extending to a mystic sense of continuity between the living and the dead,"[24] and nowhere is this more clearly expressed in McDermott's fiction than in the conclusion of *Charming Billy.* Maeve and Dennis are sitting at the dining table over tea and toast in Holtzman's little house in East Hampton. There the two are together, not alone, but in "mystic continuity" with their late spouses: "the dead were there with them. . . . Billy and Claire, not forgotten, no less mourned, but silent, for now," present, but with faces "turned away" (*CB* 142). Thus do the dead give their survivors permission to complete the trajectory of their own lives in a new marriage. Dennis and Maeve have fulfilled their respective marital vows to Claire and Billy; now they must do the same for each other. No need to debate, as do Dan Lynch and the Legion lady, which spouse takes priority; they are all part of the communion/community of the saved, with no vestige of such human imperfections as jealousy. And what about the silence of Billy and Claire, "for now"? Does that phrasing not suggest that the silence will end at some point?

With *Child of My Heart,* McDermott returns to the theme of death and the afterlife via a coming-of-age novel tracing one summer in the life of a young girl. Earlier novels have dealt with McDermott's job experience before she became a writer, her Long Island roots, her Irish American identity, and her Catholic faith. *Child of My Heart* is the first to draw on McDermott's experience as a mother of three, including detailed descriptions of the care of children, one young, the other sick, both neglected by the adults responsible for them.

CHAPTER 6

Child of My Heart (2002)

Like its four predecessors, *Child of My Heart* is structured around the nature of memory. The first-person narrator, as in *That Night,* is an adult looking back on the events of one summer. The affluent eastern Long Island beach town where fifteen-year-old Theresa works as a babysitter resembles the one in which Billy Lynch first met Eva, who, with her sister Mary, was caring for the children of the wealthy as does Theresa. As in *A Bigamist's Daughter* and *At Weddings and Wakes,* storytelling is crucial, in that the smaller narratives within the larger one, stories told by Theresa to Daisy, sound the novel's major themes. As are most of the characters in *At Weddings and Wakes* and *Charming Billy,* Theresa is Irish American, but she does not identify with "Irish Catholic Queens New York" (*CB* 32), as earlier McDermott characters do. Her family's move to the Island has raised their social status a notch or two above that of Daisy's family, the Queens Village relatives. And, although Theresa is Catholic and attends a Catholic high school, she is aware of but has not internalized sexual prohibitions, as did Billy and Dennis in *Charming Billy;* in fact she doesn't seem to think of sexuality as a moral issue at all.

As Malcolm Jones points out in his *Newsweek* review of the novel, "this may be one of the few novels about the Hamptons where the heroine isn't rich."[1] Theresa's parents, hoping to introduce their attractive daughter into a social class higher than their own, have purposefully situated her in this middle-class Long Island town because it is near the wealthier Hamptons. The disparity between the haves and the have-lesses is most obvious in the summer, when the year-round residents are reminded of their lower social status by the seasonal transients who employ them as temporary domestic help. The physical setting—already limited by being within the natural microcosm of the Island—is limited further still, as Theresa is too young to drive, so her range of motion is limited by the distance she can walk. Limiting her scope even further is the fact that she is almost always accompanied by a child or pet since she works as a babysitter and dog walker for the summer people. This plot element allows McDermott to incorporate detailed descriptions of child care, each of which is highly significant in the development of the parent characters. The novel is unique in McDermott's body of work to this point in its use of animal symbolism. Close observation of animal and human behavior is often a harsh commentary on the behavior of the humans, especially regarding the care of the young. In fiction for children and young adults, the brief lives of animals are often a young person's first experience of death. In *Child of My Heart,* repeated references to the deaths of children are even more emphatic reminders of mortality as well as heavy foreshadowings of the novel's conclusion. Care of children, care of animals, and the fragility of each point to a deeper level of meaning as Theresa engages in a symbolic battle between the forces of life and the forces of death.

The Coming of Age

Reviewer Tom Deignan calls *Child of My Heart* "a Huckleberry Finn for Irish Catholic girls."[2] Like Mark Twain's novel, it is a coming-of-age story and has many features in common with that fictional genre. The temporal setting, summertime, is typical of the young adult novel in that the protagonist's regular activities are suspended for the duration, and the change of routine opens the young person to other changes as well. In young adult fiction, the world in which the adolescent must make his or her way is one in which some adults are helpful, others hurtful, and the difference between them often unclear. Maturation is usually gender-specific in that the form adulthood takes is different for boys than it is for girls, that difference often manifesting itself in spatial terms. Huck, being a boy, has a passage to maturity that is a journey outward, as he leaves home and experiences adventures along the Mississippi River that prepare him to "light out" further still.

Theresa's story, however, is more like a fairy tale for girls than it is like Twain's quintessential boys' story. In the traditional girls' story, the function of domestic space is to provide shelter and safety. The girls' story typically begins with a young, virginal protagonist safely ensconced in her father's house but on the verge of moving into the slightly larger world of female maturity. Her movement in space is likely to be confined to a few other nearby interior spaces. Theresa's movement in space is much less confined, however, and therefore less protected. Long Island real estate, even the humbler East End homes of the less affluent, is expensive, requiring both of her parents to work full time, so Theresa's house is empty all day. Not only is she herself unsupervised but she oversees two children younger than herself. The spatial confinement typical of the fairy-tale heroine does not apply as stringently to her in that, while she must remain close to home, she has access to houses not her own because of her child care and dog walking duties. In addition, most of the plot events in *Child of My Heart* are influenced by the summer weather, "blurring property borders and even the borders between inside and outside"; the Moran children and their activities in the space between the houses and in the yard are examples of this "blurring" of boundaries.[3] All this freedom to move about in space foreshadows the moment when she will leave the artist's house for his detached studio to offer him her virginity.

Ideally, female maturation involves a smooth transition from the life of a daughter in her father's house to that of a wife in her husband's house. An even better outcome would be a move into a higher social class via marriage, and this is Theresa's parents' plan for her. Their move to the East End of Long Island from Queens is an attempt to negotiate a "marriage-plot scenario" in which their daughter will marry a Hamptons version of the handsome prince.[4] Thus, Theresa journeys from the humble abode of her upbringing (her parents' house) to variants of the prince's castle (the houses of the wealthy families for whom she pet sits, the artist's house, and, finally, his private space, his studio). But Theresa's entree into these houses is as a domestic servant, not as a social equal, and this makes a difference.

Just as in the boys' story there are ogres to be battled, in the girls' story there are forces arrayed against her, many of them subtle and ambiguous. Theresa is on her own in this environment. The adults around her are preoccupied at best and abusive at worst. Regarding the children, the adults have abdicated their responsibility.

Caring, and Not Caring, for Children

When McDermott's children were small, she adjusted her own writing time according to their needs: "I know I've got to quit writing at 2:30 because I've got to pick up the kids, and I might get back to my desk that night and I might not, and tomorrow morning they might both wake up with colds and I won't get there at all."[5] The manner in which she conformed her own schedule to that of her children contrasts with the deeply egocentric behavior of the unnamed artist and his wife in *Child of My Heart*. With his separate studio and his little staff of docile females, the artist can, especially in the light of McDermott's own reported work habits, be read as more than a bit pompous. Unconscious of his obligations as a parent, especially in the absence of his wife, he delegates all child care tasks to subordinates, only one of whom, the teenage babysitter, genuinely cares for the child. The child's mother is as self-involved as the artist is, and without any pretense of creating art. Her behavior suggests that she too assumes that a member of the lower orders will always be available to supervise her child when she does not choose to do so. Both parents shirk responsibility. But so, it appears, do most of the other parents in the novel.

The long days Theresa spends with children include many details of child-rearing and domestic life with which the novelist, as a mother, would be familiar. Daily routines are described in detail: preparing meals and snacks for Daisy and Flora, trundling Flora to the beach in her stroller, monitoring the energy levels of both children, putting them down for naps, changing them into their bathing suits on the beach. In all of these details, Theresa is "interact[ing] exclusively with children in need of adult care,"[6] taking the place of physically and psychologically absent parents. She is not, however, in charge of providing them with clothing, and clothing images are particularly effective in illustrating the relationship between children and their mothers.

Gender-biased though it may be, the way a child is dressed, especially a girl child, is a fairly reliable barometer of a mother's attention and judgment. At minimum, children's clothing must be clean, and they must be dressed correctly for the time of day, for the activity, and for the weather. The next-door children, the Morans, are not. They are often inappropriately dressed for the season, dirty, wearing the previous day's clothes, and—in the case of baby June, a toddler—a diaper long overdue for a change. Daisy, child of an overburdened mother, is clean but is sent away for the summer, unaccompanied on the Long Island Railroad, in "new, cheap clothes that Theresa recognizes immediately as the caste marker of a family that is unable to control its reproductive urges."[7] Not only are the clothes low in quality, they are so large that they are obviously meant to accommodate the following summer, a summer that will not come for Daisy. The age-arranged clothing that Theresa's mother has stored in the attic, a veritable museum of her past, is oddly incompatible with the mother's seeming detachment from Theresa in the present. Daisy's willingness to wear Theresa's dresses not only compensates for Daisy's mother's lack of care in assembling a summer wardrobe for her but also provides an indicator of her desire to emulate Theresa. Flora's white dresses, lovely but impractical on an active toddler (especially one being allowed to drink red Hawaiian Punch), indicates her mother's interest in her more as an accessory in a fashion shoot than as a flesh-and-blood child. These mothers provide inadequate care for their children and an inadequate set of role models for Theresa.

In a traditional coming-of-age story, the young girl must be initiated into womanhood, and the form that this initiation will take is determined by the culture. Theresa is a bright, creative high school student, a reader and a teller of tales, clearly capable of assuming a variety of roles in the larger world. Her activities during this particular summer, however, are restricted to the domestic sphere. Her parents, "children of immigrants, well-read but undereducated" (*CH* 13), make no college-preparatory summer plans for Theresa, and "no one mentions her intellect as a route to success and fulfillment."[8] This despite the fact that Theresa is clearly an intelligent young woman, one of McDermott's most well-read protagonists, albeit in high school curriculum authors like Shakespeare, Thomas Hardy, Edgar Allan Poe, and Mark Twain. Her education is experiential that summer, consisting of meeting a variety of potential adult role models, all of whom illuminate the adult world she is about to enter. That summer Theresa "negotiates the divide between the world of children and that of adults, a gap made perilous by the irresponsibility of parents."[9] Since she is expected to fill a gender-specific role, she must first look to the women around her for guidance in how to live.

It is a truism that an "adult female mentor" is needed for a girl's "healthy emotional and psychological maturation."[10] Theresa's mother, her primary mentor, reserves the bulk of her attention for her husband. A shadowy figure, lightly characterized, she leaves for work early every morning, comes home late, and interacts little with her daughter. This tangential relationship with Theresa leaves the young girl alone with her developing problems. Fifteen-year-old girls appear to be, and in some ways are, mature, as suggested by the common custom of allowing them to babysit younger children. But adolescents can have little experience of the world upon which to base serious decision-making. This becomes apparent with Daisy's recurrent bruising, a worrisome symptom. Responsibility for a child's health is far beyond the scope of a teenage babysitter's capability. As the adult on the premises, Theresa's mother should be monitoring the situation since, if the bruises are visible to Theresa and to Dr. Kaufman, they must be visible to her as well. The mother of a teenage girl should also be attuned to the fact (as the men of the Hamptons certainly are) that her beautiful daughter is on the brink of adult sexuality and should take some care concerning her associations. Her "benign neglect,"[11] and that of her husband, has serious consequences.

Another significant woman in Theresa's life is her Aunt Peg, Daisy's mother, who delegates full-time, round-the-clock care of her young and, as it turns out, sick child to a teenager. Aunt Peg's situation is an example of a common McDermott theme: the relationship of social class to various Long Island neighborhoods. The family lives in Queens Village, a neighborhood with even less prestige than that in which Theresa and her family live. Raising a family on the single salary of a transit police officer, Aunt Peg—a long-suffering mother of too many children and her life chaotic because of her uncontrolled fertility—begrudges Theresa's family their lifestyle, as if their relative comfort was purchased at her expense. Her slapdash care of Daisy, indicated by the thoughtless way in which she assembles the child's clothes for the summer, is not necessarily solely due to a limited budget. Theresa would not know whether the unmanageably large family is a result of Daisy's parents' adherence to Catholic prohibitions on birth control or mere fecklessness. But anyone who grew up Catholic at the time would have known one of these families, or been a member of one, without enough money or time for all those children. It would take an unusual woman to manage such a large family, and Aunt Peg is relentlessly ordinary.

Both these women affect Theresa's life more by what they do not do than what they do. Like her father, Theresa's mother acts as if she believes that all she needs to do is place her daughter in proximity to wealthy men in the Hamptons. Aunt Peg has no options for her daughter's summer than to accept a free offer of a full-time babysitter. Theresa does not report any discussion of alternative plans for the summer other than to put the two cousins together and let them fend for themselves. This maternal disengagement has serious consequences for both girls.

In addition to these two key mother figures, other lightly sketched but significant peripheral female characters offer Theresa a glimpse into her possible futures. The artist's wife, beautiful like Theresa, is the trophy of an older, famous, wealthy man, and she lives in just such a manner as Theresa's parents seem to desire for her. The artist's wife's casual approach to arranging care for her toddler daughter is evidence of her indifference to the child and to her role as mother, suggesting that the main function of the child is to tie her fortunes more firmly to those of the artist. She has staff, a housekeeper and a cook, to free her from domestic tasks, but she does not use that time to care for her child. Her abandonment of the child to the staff and to Theresa after an argument with her husband is a measure of her carelessness. She is neither happy nor productive, and her child, while competently overseen by the babysitter, is clearly neglected by her parents. The housekeeper, who clearly regards care for Flora as not her job, deposits the toddler on the porch strapped into her stroller, as if she were a package to be picked up. An alert parent reading the novel would note how irresponsible this is, in that the safe handoff of the baby to the sitter is by no means guaranteed. Wealthy people, if they choose not to care for their child themselves, can certainly provide a better child care arrangement than this.

The other members of the artist's domestic staff include Ana, the housekeeper/substitute sex partner, and the cook, a local woman who comes in by the day. Dr. Kaufman's wife unknowingly provides sex education for Theresa via her impromptu, noisy encounter with her husband within Theresa's earshot.

That wife is easily replaced by Dr. Kaufman's vapid new girlfriend, Jill, whose halfhearted introduction to the Kaufman twins is facilitated by Theresa. The household of Theresa's next-door neighbors, the Morans, "unruly shanty Irish,"[12] is disorderly, featuring transient men, drunkenness, and drama. The children's mother, Sondra, another careless procreator, delegates responsibility for baby June to her not-much-older siblings and to Theresa, who, unofficially and unpaid, keeps a casual eye on them. As Mary Paniccia Carden observes, throughout the novel "adults tend to treat children like afterthoughts and burdens."[13] During this formative summer of her life, Theresa is influenced by these inferior specimens of adult womanhood.

What is true of the women is even more true of the men. When Daisy seems feverish, Theresa doses her with St. Joseph's Aspirin for Children. The repetition of this particular brand name is not mere product placement but a reminder of the husband of Mary and father of Jesus, whose role in Catholic lore is as paragon of male virtue. To a man like the artist, the chaste Joseph is no more than a "poor schmuck" (*CH* 223), and the other men in Theresa's world are no match for the Josephite ideal either. Daisy's father, Uncle Jack, the transit cop, obsessive enforcer of rules, is a comic figure satirizing male authoritarianism. Theresa's father is a good person, albeit like her mother shadowy and detached; his main function in the novel appears to be supplying first aid for Daisy's injury. The drunken grandfather and the various men in the next-door Moran household suggest that men are at best useless, at worst dangerous, in any case temporary. For all their defects, these men are peripheral to Theresa's life, neither helping or hindering her on her passage to adulthood.

More ambiguous in his influence on Theresa is Dr. Kaufman. He takes an interest in Daisy, notices her bruises, and suggests that Theresa follow up with the child's parents and physician. As a physician himself and a father, however, he should be well aware of the foolhardiness of entrusting responsibility for a child's health to a teenage babysitter. Minimally, if he suspected signs of illness, abuse, or neglect, Dr. Kaufman should insist on discussing the matter at least with Theresa's parents, ideally with Daisy's parents. It seems as if Daisy's bruises are at least partially an excuse for him to have continued conversation with Theresa. He is not a bad man, but he is flawed in being negligent about Daisy and, on several occasions, flirtatious with Theresa. In the latter behavior, he foreshadows her relationship with the artist.

One of the novel's many ironies is that Theresa's parents are blind to the reality that all their "romantic plotting" has left their daughter "vulnerable" to the likes of the artist.[14] A summer of child care has effectively removed her from the presence of boys her own age; her nascent romantic feelings thus attach themselves to an unsuitable object, the artist. Theresa, looking back as an adult, remembers herself at the time as making a conscious decision regarding their eventual sexual encounter. But New York State age of consent laws during the time in which the novel takes place are clear. There are few references to events in the outside world in the novel on which to situate the present-time action. At one point, however, Theresa and Daisy visit a Horn and Hardart's Automat on a trip to Manhattan, which means the action is set before 1991, when the last such restaurant closed, but after the deaths of Marilyn Monroe in 1962 and Jayne Mansfield in 1967. Between 1920 and 2006, the age of consent was eighteen, lowered to seventeen in 2007, but at no point in the twentieth century was it lower. There are also legal restrictions on the permissible age disparity between the adult and the underage person: no more than four years.

Ironically, although Theresa protects children and pets, she cannot protect herself from "the principal male predator of the novel."[15] She apparently believed herself at the time to have agency in this matter, but the law says otherwise: she is not considered legally competent to consent. Though no force is used, this is a rape, a "grotesque parody of her parents' dream."[16] The narrator, long an adult, "never actually states that she was a victim of statutory rape by the artist when she was fifteen,"[17] so deeply has she hidden this fact even from herself. But why would Theresa ever have believed that she consented to an act that seems "inexplicable."[18] An explanation lies in her imagining herself as a warrior against death, and the imagery of animals and of dying and dead children are intricately connected with this self-perception.

The Cosmic Battle: Love and Death in the Hamptons

The novel begins in late August, flashes back to the beginning of the summer, and ends in the same late August, the death knell of summer, with Daisy returned to her parents and to futile medical treatment. All summer, the life and death of animals and children are connected with Daisy's situation, which in turn leads to Theresa's perceiving herself as engaged in a battle against death. Each animal, and each story of a dead or dying child, fulfills a distinct role in reinforcing these key themes of the novel.

Rupert and Angus, the Richardsons' Scotties, are the least problematic of these animals as they are substitutes for the couple's dead child and are accordingly treasured. The Kaufmans' dog, Red Rover, has owners who are not home enough to have a dog at all, but at least they outsource him to a responsible and loving caretaker. The stray animals adopted by the Moran children are like the children themselves, neglected, "probably left behind by some summer people who didn't want the year-round responsibility of a pet; occasionally . . . adopted by another summer family who made him theirs for whatever time they were out here" (*CH* 83). Rags is the most significant of them—at once most the most endangered (the Moran children's grandfather threatens to shoot him) and the most dangerous (he bites Daisy, in consequence of which her illness is discovered and her summer idyll ended). Even his name suggests that he is a castoff, like the stray cat known as Garbage.

The trio of cats, Moe, Larry, and Curly, are summer pets, rented by the Swansons for the summer along with the house so that their children can "have the experience of pets without the year-long obligation" (*CH* 51), an "obligation" that would of course be that of the parents, not of young children. A transient in the life of the child Debbie Swanson, Curly, provides the child with her first experience of mortality, as pets often do. "This is why I never wanted them," her mother says (*CH* 158), as if keeping the child away from animals could stave off death. Debbie's refusal to "let go" of the dead cat (*CH* 153), her insistence against all evidence that the cat can be saved, parallels Theresa's reluctance to report the clear signs of Daisy's illness. Most significant concerning the unfortunate Curly is Theresa's response to his death: "It was the worst thing. It was *what I was up against*" (*CH* 169; my italics). Theresa's sense of herself as a warrior against death explains why she is so emotionally involved with the baby rabbits; two descriptions of her rescuing the rabbits begin and end the novel.

The rabbits enter the novel as the objects of Petey Moran's futile quest to demonstrate his love for Daisy, then modulate into a potent symbol of the fragility of life. Theresa tries to save them, but her efforts are similar to the twig holding up the rabbit trap, "something slight and fragile holding back a weighty darkness" (*CH* 158). Her battle with that "weighty darkness" competes with her understanding that the rabbits were "not meant to live, as my parents had told me, being wild things" (*CH* 3). Her gesture in making a nest for them, a substitute womb, by lining an empty box with grass and placing them in it, is an attempt to maintain the lives of these "hopeless little things" (*CH* 242). Here McDermott captures the point in time in which a young girl discovers simultaneously her need to love and care for the weak and helpless and the pain that need will cause her in the future the "inevitable, insufferable loss buried like a dark jewel at the heart of every act of love" (*CH* 242).

Theresa's behavior in several of her less rational choices makes more sense once the significance of her behavior with the rabbits is established. Theresa has overstepped her authority in giving Daisy aspirin to combat her fevers (with no regard for appropriate dosage) and in failing to report the fevers, the bruising, the unusual fatigue. It is not surprising that one so young would be immature, and inexperience accounts for "her denial of adult advice and her inability to see the consequences of her having delayed an intervention."[19] Her motivations are complex: adolescent hubris; concern for Daisy's enjoyment of the summer; and defiance in the face of death—the enemy she is "up against" (*CH* 169). Warrior against death, she believes, against all reason, that her love for Daisy can overcome mortality itself. Paradoxically, that irrational belief also explains her having sex with the artist. On the plot level, this encounter defies probability. The adult Theresa, narrating the episode, seems to remember only mild erotic curiosity, not even amounting to attraction. This apparently unmotivated incident, however, is another response to the forces of death that lurk just below the surface of Theresa's Long Island Eden.

Child of My Heart is a meditation on the precariousness and fragility of life. The Kaufmans' Red Rover is the lone remnant of a family's lost unity; the Richardsons' dogs Angus and Rupert replace their dead son; Curly the cat's violent death traumatizes a child. The death of animals in children's literature (as in, for example, E. B. White's *Charlotte's Web*) introduces children to mortality, usually accompanied by parental reassurance that death comes to all, even the child, but in the far, far distant future. In *Child of My Heart,* the stakes are much higher because the death of Daisy takes place in March following this summer idyll, and Theresa the adult narrator sees all the events of the summer through the lens of that tragedy.

Daisy's name, like all flower images, is a conventional reminder of the evanescence of life, and the many references to dying and dead children heavily foreshadow Daisy's own passing. Theresa discovers that she once had a stillborn baby brother, named Robert Emmet after the Irish patriot; now Theresa realizes that she is not an only child but a surviving child with a dead sibling. This makes her identify with Daisy's sister, Bernadette, who will one day need to learn to live without her sister. The dead children in the stories within the main narrative—the ghost child in the attic; the child whose death is commemorated annually by the bereaved parents' decorating a tree with lollipops; the little girl dead in her First Communion slip; Macduff's children in *Macbeth,* all murdered; the Richardsons' dead child, Andrew Thomas, frozen in time by the childhood photograph; Theresa's lost baby brother—all foreshadow what lies ahead for Daisy.

Daisy senses that, like the crewmen in the old song that she and Theresa paraphrase to make it more optimistic, she will never return to the scenes of this summer's joys. Theresa's violent emotional response synthesizes all the imagery of dead and dying children and of animals:

> a flash of black anger . . . suddenly made me want to kick those damn cats off the bed and banish every parable, every song, every story ever told, even by me, about children who never returned. The newborn children named for Irish patriots. The children who said, I want to show it to the angels.

> Children who kissed their toys at night and said, Wait for me, who dreamt lollipop trees, who bid farewell to their parents from the evening star, who took to heart an old man's advice that they never grow old, and never did. All my pretty ones? All? (*CH* 179–80).

The pervasive imagery of death and dying in a novel about a teenager's summer job explains Theresa's motivation for sex with the artist. The young man with the notebook, apparently someone writing about the artist and who is identified at once with Satan the Tempter and with Shakespeare's Macduff, he who lost "all" his "pretty" children, appears abruptly to offer a key piece of information, then disappears. The artist, says he, will not be satisfied with the "middle-aged and plump" Ana, the housekeeper. He needs "something young and lively . . . child-bearing, for dessert. . . . It's a 'blood-of-a-virgin' kind of thing" (*CH* 188). The visitor plants in Theresa's mind the idea that, for the artist, sex is an affirmation of life in the face of death; so, since she perceives herself as a warrior against death, the next step makes emotional if not logical sense. Paradoxically, she has sex with the artist not because she loves him but because she loves Daisy and knows on some level that the child will be lost.

As the narrator looks back at this crucial experience from the perspective of middle age, she does not seem to acknowledge that her motivation might have involved the possible conception of a new child. A new baby, however inconveniently timed, strikes a blow for life and against death. The reader never knows—the adult Theresa does not divulge—whether a pregnancy resulted from that single act and, if so, what became of the child. But it is common for McDermott to leave such serious issues unresolved. It is possible that having sex with the artist, whose procreative potential is confirmed by the existence of Flora, is Theresa's instinctive attempt to replace Daisy, thus "conquering" death by leaving herself open to the forces of life.

The relationship between women and girls and young children illustrated so well in this novel will take center stage in McDermott's next novel, *After This.* In no other novel thus far has McDermott concentrated in such detail on the female body, especially the physical sensations of pregnancy and childbearing. But, concerned as she always is with the spirit as well as the flesh, McDermott will also develop a theology of maternity.

CHAPTER 7

After This (2006)

Mary, the protagonist of *After This,* thirty and single, seems destined for a life as a traditional "old girl" in her father's household, keeping house for her father and brother, going to church, toiling in the steno pool. The time as the novel begins is the 1950s and the place, McDermott's typical Brooklyn/Queens/Nassau County area. Neither the time nor the place would be a prime locus for a radical redefinition of women's role, and Mary does not imagine any options other than her life as it is, or marriage. She prays not for rescue but for the fortitude to "be content" (*AT* 4), to accept that her life, even as a single woman, is "not so bad" (*AT* 16). A rainy, windy day introduces one of this complex novel's themes: the uncontrollable aspects of life to which Mary is exposed once she ventures forth from the relative security of a simple life. The wind causes Mary to strike up conversations with two men, one of whom she will later marry. Wind imagery modulates thereafter into a continuing meditation on the nature of motherhood. Alice McDermott's experience as mother of three, which shapes the child care details in *Child of My Heart,* is on display here also, with dimensions from the physical, to the psychological, to the spiritual. Natural symbolism (rain, the ocean, beach sand, and especially wind) conveys the terrifying risk involved in parenthood. The third-person narrator describes women's physical experiences, the sensations of pregnancy, childbirth, and abortion, in vivid detail. At the same time, the child-free life is also presented as a desirable alternative. Finally, the theology of motherhood is explored through the pervasive reminders throughout the novel of Jesus's mother, also a woman named Mary.

"Once More into the Breach": Daring Parenthood

Mary's walking out of church and into a windstorm is a perfect metaphor for leaving the celibate life for marriage and parenthood. Bad weather triggers Mary's conversation, first with her brother's friend George, then with John Keane. George's physical reaction to the weather—"his eyes were teary from the wind, red-rimmed and bloodshot" (*AT* 5)—makes him appear vulnerable. But John uses the wind to self-satirize, to play at being the soldier he once was, returning to do battle with the storm: "'Once more into the breach,' he said, turning up his collar. 'Wish me luck'" (*AT* 8). His limp shows that he has been wounded, and, though some women would find this disheartening, to Mary the limp means that he has faced challenges and survived. This scene establishes the wind as one of several significant "echoes . . . recursive phrases" upon which the novel is built.[1]

Mary's instincts from that chance meeting are correct in leading her to John Keane. He does in fact step into the breach, filling the empty space in Mary's life as a considerate lover, a good husband, a responsible father, a dependable wage-earner. However, by the time of Mary's pregnancy with their fourth and final child, Clare, John is experiencing fatherhood as a burden: "His love for his children bore down on his heart with the weight of three heavy stones" (*AT* 35). While Mary carries the physical weight of this baby, John bears the weight of his own anxiety. His brother Frank's sudden death of a heart attack has made him aware of the fragility of his own life, especially in terms of the potential impact of his death on his daughter. He has been profoundly affected by giving away his niece at her marriage; he fears dying before his daughter Annie is married and therefore hopes the new baby will be a boy. Having persuaded Mary on one windy September Sunday to seize the day, to "skip Mass just this once and head to the beach" (*AT* 29), he feels himself, at fifty-one, in the September of his own life as well.

Jones Beach on the south shore of Long Island is empty that day because it is after Labor Day, that wistful valedictory to summer. The wind is a constant, variable presence, ominous, portending a worse dose of weather to come.[2] Early that morning, the wind had awakened John, reminding him of his wartime experience. Later, on the beach, the wind is unkind to him as it "lifted his . . . thinning hair" (*AT* 29), another *memento mori*. The wind affects all the senses: the sand hits the skin like tiny arrows; the beach grass "shuddered" (*AT* 33); voices are blown away across the empty beach so that the parents occasionally feel uneasy about the children's whereabouts. John's desire to protect his family is demonstrated by his repeatedly urging them, especially pregnant Mary, to shelter from the wind to which, ironically, his own beach plan has exposed them. Altogether, the winds that in the earlier chapter were invitations to join in life's multifarious adventures here become the threats that surround the Keane family, threats of which John is most keenly aware.

When the family has returned home and should be safe, the wind worsens. A major storm threatens to uproot a tree on their property large enough to destroy their home and even kill them. John's responsibility as husband and father is to protect his family despite his own fear, which he experiences as chest sensations mimicking the heart attack from which Frank died. So great is his fear of death that he imagines that the fireman who comes to warn the family of the tree's imminent collapse is a supernatural death messenger and the wind, the cry of the banshee. Under John's direction, the family retreats to their basement, where they safely listen to the wind and are protected from the fall of the tree. This scene reappears in Annie's memory when, studying abroad in England as a young college student, she hears Professor Wallace's narrative of her own experience as a child during World War II. Her grandmother hid her and her cousins in a cellar during an air raid; more adept than John in coping with life-threatening emergencies, she insisted that the children be separated from each other and "scattered to different corners of the cellar, in case . . . some part of the ceiling came down, not, one would hope, on us all" (*AT* 239). When Annie leaves her family to make a new life in London with her boyfriend, the image of the children in the basement convinces her of "the wisdom of scattering" family members across the world, "each to a different corner of whatever shelter they had found, so that should the worst happen, happen again, it would not take them all" (*AT* 251). All three scenes stress the fearful weight of responsibility and terror of loss that is the consequence of love for family.

And the wind, the multitude of threats that it symbolizes, will always return. Mr. Persichetti, a neighbor who is a nurse and who appears at crisis points, is often described as wearing a "Windbreaker" (*AT* 204), badge of his role as protector, and he does come to Mary Keane's rescue when she goes into labor unexpectedly. But the family cannot always be protected. When, years later, Jacob picks up Clare from school to take her for a final car ride before he leaves for Vietnam, "there seemed to be a constant wind blowing . . . full of sand and grit" (*AT* 142), the imagery echoing that of the beach episode. To marry and have children is to find fulfillment, but also to risk irremediable loss. When Jacob is killed in Vietnam. Mary tells Pauline that she will "never get over it." Pauline could have replied platitudinously, "yes, you will," but instead responds truly: "I don't expect you will" (*AT* 207). Pauline, often more of a liability than an asset to the Keane family, here does Mary a service by acknowledging a mother's grief, a grief that the childless woman will never experience.

In Love and In Trouble: The Female Body

The contrast between these two women, one a wife and mother, the other a lifelong virgin, is not just symbolic but physical. More than McDermott's previous novels, *After This* focuses considerable attention on female anatomy. The physiology of virginity, the sensations of pregnancy and childbirth, the experience of abortion, and the possibility of death of a mother or baby in childbirth all figure prominently in the novel.

Virginity must be understood against the background of the high value placed on the intact female body in the Catholic religious tradition. As an article of faith, Mary, Jesus's mother, is believed to have conceived and birthed her son while preserving her virginity. McDermott's novel takes no theological position on this doctrine. She does, however, gently satirize the Catholic glorification of the virginal state via the story of Saint Dymphna, which Mr. Persichetti tells Mary while she is in labor. This tale belongs to a category of Catholic story called the *vita,* or saint's life, a devotional genre that presents its mostly apocryphal protagonists as models for proper Christian behavior. Many of these stories involve assaults on the integrity of the female body: rape or attempted rape, torture, mutilation, dismemberment. Dymphna's fate has the additional titillating feature of incestuous sex. Daughter of a pagan father and a Christian mother, the lovely Dymphna is the object of her mad father's lust. After he tries to "marry" her, she escapes but was probably (according to Mr. Persichetti) pursued by her father and decapitated. The *vitae* are typically even more improbable than this one, and often just as ambiguous. On one level, the story of the saint exalts female chastity, but on another level, it also implicitly condones a sadistic contemplation of the violated female body. Mary and Mr. Persichetti, cradle Catholics familiar with this particular form of religious absurdity, can see the dark humor in the tale of the doomed Dymphna.

Virginity for the Keane family, however, is neither a life-and-death matter nor a litmus test of virtue. Mary Keane abandoned her virginity early and casually ("she thought, Why not" [*AT* 9]), and feels sorry for Pauline because she preserved hers. Unlike the nuns who will be depicted in *The Ninth Hour,* Pauline is not a consecrated virgin, a status that commands respect in the Catholic tradition. Pauline's virginity is by default, indicating a failure to engage with life, to step out in the wind as did Mary. Except for Clare, who loves Pauline, the Keanes usually see Pauline as falling somewhere on the spectrum from a "royal pain in the ass" (*AT* 78) to a madwoman in the attic (though Annie confuses the caretaker in Charlotte Brontë's *Jane Eyre,* Grace Poole, with the actual madwoman, Bertha Rochester [*AT* 197]). On the other hand, the single, child-free life has its perquisites, at least as it is perceived by a child-harried mother. At one point, when picking up Clare, for whom Pauline had been baby-sitting, Mary "looked at [Pauline's] peaceful rooms with some envy," thinking about the annoyances of the day and the "bedtime routine that was still waiting for her at home" (*AT* 102). But ordinarily Pauline's life in the "spinster chorus" (*AT* 15) is seen as sometimes pitiful, sometimes a source of prurient humor. When Mary takes Pauline to the gynecologist, the doctor must break her hymen in order to complete the examination, and Annie, hearing this, is distressed. Later Annie will hear the group at Professor Wallace's house mock the novelist Edith Wharton, who, though married, was a virgin until commencing a love affair at age forty-five. In general, the physical state of virginity, when not undertaken in religious life, is seen as an act of omission rather than a conscious commitment.

Marriage without children is an option personified by Professor Elizabeth Wallace. To Annie, a young student exposed to a different culture and social class for the first time, Professor Wallace seems to be a role model worth emulating. With her lovely home, her handsome husband, her successful academic career, and her general air of literary sophistication, Professor Wallace is an example of what the child-free life can be. Without children, one can entertain elegantly, engage in witty chatter uninterrupted, drink good wine, cultivate an aura of superiority. As a mother, McDermott well knows that this life is, at least temporarily, not possible while raising children. For Annie, at a stage in which she must build an identity separate from her family, part of the attraction of imitating Professor Wallace, of "growing literary and worldly-wise, nearly British" (*AT* 224), is that it would give her a life different from her mother's, from that of any mother.

Mary's last pregnancy and abrupt delivery are described in physiologically accurate detail. During the windy day at the beach, Mary experiences typical sensations of late pregnancy: "She felt the baby ripple under her fingers. She felt a heel—surely it was a heel here on her left side—press against her skin and then dart away, going under, before she could quite gauge its shape" (*AT* 37). The suddenness of Clare's birth is likewise described graphically: the sensation of water breaking, the pain of unmedicated labor, the fear (in those days before the duration of pregnancy was routinely monitored by sonography; before the care of premature infants had pushed back the limits of viability) that a six-weeks-premature baby would likely not survive. Metaphorically, but also literally, Mary has opened herself up to this intense experience once she stepped out into the wind. When, some years later, Mary sees Michelangelo's Pietà at the 1964 World's Fair in Flushing, Mary notices how the position of Mary in the sculpture, of the Virgin's open legs as she holds her dead son, echoes the position of a woman in childbirth—an image far more explicit than is traditionally associated with Jesus's mother.

Susan Persichetti's abortion is also described in graphic detail and with emotional sensitivity. The orthodox Catholic position on abortion is represented by Sister Lucy, who commemorates the anniversary of *Roe v. Wade*, the 1973 Supreme Court decision legalizing abortion in the United States, by comparing women who terminate their pregnancies to Euripides's Medea, revenge killer of her own children. Sister Lucy's literary analogy is problematic. While Medea's agency in the murders is undeniable, Euripides also places responsibility on Jason, whose utterly obtuse argument is that he is marrying a well-connected younger woman so that he and Medea's children will benefit from the higher-status stepbrothers Jason plans to engender upon his new young wife. But Sister Lucy lets Jason off the hook completely and similarly makes no mention of the male role in unplanned pregnancy. The injustice of it all is stressed in Euripides by the fact that Jason's new bride also dies at Medea's hands while Jason, though bereaved of his sons, is free to find yet another woman and have yet more sons. Such are nature's injustices, compounded by human choices.

Ironically, if Susan Persichetti, whose boyfriend escapes responsibility for the unplanned pregnancy, had pursued birth control with the same efficiency with which she arranges for her abortion, she might have avoided the pregnancy. Susan does not consciously see the abortion decision as being a moral choice so much as a practical one: her main goal is to get back to her ordinary life as a college-bound high school senior. Her determination does not mitigate her fear of the procedure itself, described in precise medical detail: "Inside, Susan gave a urine sample and then undressed and was examined, and when the pregnancy was confirmed, the procedure was explained to her. The strange words: cervix and uterus, dilation and curettage, felt like a steel blade against the edge of her teeth" (*AT* 156–57). The abortion is painful, and Susan's reaction is conflicted. She recites a Catholic prayer expressing sorrow for sin, the "Act of Contrition," as if after a sacramental confession. At the same time she also feels relieved that she has, as she planned, "gotten through" (*AT* 158) the crisis that could have derailed her plans.

Regarding an unexpected teen pregnancy, Clare is the antithesis of Susan. She is just the kind of young girl at that time who would find herself pregnant in high school. The extent of her sex education is a cautionary film on childbirth shown to young girl students and obviously intended to "terrify them into chastity": "In health class that fall, they'd been shown a film: a hospital birth, the woman red-faced and panting, her pale, raised knees, more blood and less privacy than any of them had imagined. A scalpel moving in for what they called the episiotomy. . . . Girls with their hands over their mouths stumbled from the room" (*AT* 267). What is missing from the lesson, this being a Catholic school, is contraception. Neither Clare nor Gregory have even dated before, and neither are prepared for a responsible adult sexual relationship. Even if they had known how to procure birth control and use it, to two young Catholics at the time, doing so would make the sex act seem premeditated and therefore even more sinful than an impetuous coupling might be. Having become pregnant, Clare never considers abortion; rather, she exists in a state of dreamy denial for months before telling her parents. Her inaction constitutes a decision to continue the pregnancy.

The response of all concerned is stereotypical. Gregory, the accidental father, is shocked and annoyed; Mary slaps her daughter's face; both she and John insist on a confrontational meeting with Gregory's parents. At this meeting, accusations of rape and seduction are traded, and adoption is suggested; no one suggests Clare's raising the child on her own. But neither do they exile her from the community, as was the fate of Sheryl in *That Night*. Soon Gregory, influenced by a priest, accepts responsibility, which for him involves quitting college and getting a job to support his new wife and baby. The young couple plans to live in the Keanes' basement and let Grandma Mary and Pauline babysit so that Clare can go to college. The immature parents-to-be are poised to enter their own windstorm of parenthood, starting their life together via a valid, though hastily arranged and ritually truncated, Catholic marriage.

Mother of God: Mary as Feminine Ideal

Catholic language, as has been discussed regarding *Charming Billy,* reappears in *After This* as scriptural references and formal prayers. Churchgoing, even if sporadic, fixes words and phrases in memory, to be called to consciousness at the merest allusion. Biblical passages, especially because they are intended for oral delivery, feature simple, memorable sensory images that convey a clear didactic message. Other nonliturgical prayers, such as "Angel of God," recited by the Keane family for protection from the storm (*AT* 52), have traditionally been memorized in Catholic schools. Belief may waver or fade, but these words remain. Another element of McDermott's style involves the short phrases, in effect microprayers, interjected into casual conversation. All this repetition establishes a habit of prayer in the cradle Catholics of *After This:* John ponders the relationship of prayer to immortality; Jacob prays for his own safety; Michael remembers a formulaic prayer at a most unusual time; Susan Persichetti, postabortion, prays for absolution. All these influences give McDermott's prose style "an almost liturgical rhythm."[3]

In *After This,* because of the novel's focus on women, prayers to Jesus's mother, Mary, are particularly significant. The title of the novel is taken from a well-known prayer to the Blessed Virgin, the *Salve Regina,* "Hail Holy Queen." The single phrase "after this" triggers a memory of the rest of the prayer: "after this our exile, show unto us the blessed fruit of thy womb, Jesus. Holy Mary, Mother of God, pray for us sinners, now and at the hour of our death. Amen." "This"—life on earth—is exile, imperfection, incompleteness, compared to the perfect happiness achievable "after this," in heaven, the spirit's true home. This prayer will recur and be expanded upon at an unexpected point in the novel, as Michael Keane implores the aid of his heavenly Mother. In Catholic teaching, Mary is a maternal version of divinity, her qualities mirroring what were thought to be appropriate female characteristics at the time, such as caring for her people as a mother would her children. References to Jesus's mother throughout *After This* range from traditional Marian nomenclature, to references to objects of veneration related to Mary, to Marian iconography, to brief petitions in the form of short prayers, to longer formal prayers describing Mary's role in Catholicism, to the practical applications of the imitation of Mary in the daily life of the Catholic Christian woman. All this emphasis on Catholicism's most important woman intensifies the novel's theme of motherhood.

Naming customs in Catholic life are intended to encourage devotion to and imitation of the saint after whom one is named. Institutions are likewise named in praise of Mary. Clare attends Mary Immaculate High School, its name stressing Mary's sinlessness, and especially her perpetual virginity, considered a salutary lesson for young Catholic girls. Objects of veneration such as the Miraculous Medal ring that Mary wears, which belonged to her mother, are intended to cultivate Marian devotion. As in the medieval cathedrals, sculpture, stained glass, and painting teach specific doctrines; the painting of Our Lady of Perpetual Help in the old church and the name of the church itself both remind the churchgoer of Mary's supportive role. Aesthetic quality being secondary to fervency of devotion, religious kitsch can serve the same purpose as high art. The picture of the Virgin Mary painted on a neighborhood garage door, which catches the attention of Clare and Jacob on their final car ride together, may be, in the eyes of the believer if not of the art critic, as much a source of grace as a statue by Michelangelo.

References to Marian art culminate in the scene in which Mary and Annie view Michelangelo's Pietà. The sculpture, dating from 1499, depicts the sorrowing mother holding her dead son in her arms. Such a work as this is not so much intended to teach doctrine as to foster affective spirituality, an emotional response like that of the "woman . . . weeping" (*AT* 101) at the sight of the statue. At the Flushing World's Fair, the commonplace world (the heat, the long lines to the exhibit, the moving walkway, the excessive air conditioning) is the occasion of a spiritual experience: "Here was the lifeless flesh of the beloved child, the young man's muscle and sinew impossibly—impossible for the mother who cradled him—still. Here were her knees against the folds of her draped robes, her lap, as wide as it might have been in childbirth, accommodating his weight once more. Here were her fingers pressed into his side, her shoulder raised to bear him on her arm once more. Here was her left hand, open, empty. Here were the mother's eyes cast down upon the body of her child once more, only once more, and in another moment (they were moving back into the darkness) no more" (*AT* 100–1). Not only does the passage express emotions that are themselves a form of prayer but it also uses a stylistic technique from a particular form of prayer: the litany.

A litany is a series of petitions in repetitive parallel grammatical structure, with variations. For example, "The Litany of the Blessed Virgin Mary" contained in the 1956 edition of the *Saint Joseph Daily Missal* reads in part as follows: "Holy Mary, pray for us. / Holy Mother of God, pray for us. / Holy Virgin of Virgins, pray for us." This is followed by a long series of petitions addressing Mary by her various titles, such as: "Queen of Angels, pray for us. Queen of Patriarchs, pray for us. Queen of Prophets, pray for us." In McDermott's description of the Pietà, the repetition with variation of the phrases "Here were . . . here were," and "Once more . . . no more" suggest the litany form. In focusing her attention, albeit briefly considering that the moving walkway prevents extended contemplation, Mary Keane has a spiritual experience. Her awareness that the sculptor's positioning of Mary is similar to that of a birthing woman causes her to empathize with Jesus's mother's suffering in a specifically female way. The unusual nature of this insight is perhaps also a way of highlighting the way Catholicism is largely defined by men and in terms of men's bodies. The encounter with the statue also foreshadows Mary Keane's loss of her own beloved son in Vietnam.

One of McDermott's signature techniques is to juxtapose the sublime and the ridiculous. In another scene in the novel, the way women and men see religious devotion differently receives comic treatment. It was the custom for a brief interval in the long history of the Catholic Church to build new churches with a facility for isolating parents with small children to "what Father McShane [the pastor] seemed delighted to call the 'Bawl Room,' a soundproof room for mothers with small, noisy children" (*AT* 109). The Church hierarchy, perceiving no irony, regards children as a distraction, and therefore isolates them and their mothers—all the while mandating not only the mothers' attendance at Mass but also their repeated childbearing. Statues of Mary feature prominently in Catholic churches, but Mary herself would be unwelcome if she had her baby in tow. Mary Keane registers the incongruity; she "imagined the Blessed Mother with baby Jesus in her arms, standing behind the plate glass, the child's mouth moving but not a sound getting through" (*AT* 110), excluded from modern Catholic liturgical practice by this unfortunate trend in church architecture.

Habits of speech characteristic of these Irish American Catholics attest to their devotion to Mary, sometimes in decidedly secular contexts. Brief prayers, called ejaculations in Catholic terminology, are voiced by Mary Keane in labor as she calls upon Jesus's mother Mary: "Mother of God" (*AT* 67). Given the secular meaning of the term "ejaculation," Michael's friend Bean's exclamation upon seeing the naked Caroline in Damien's bar—"Mother of Mercy" (*AT* 181)—is a bit of irreverent sexual/religious word play. Longer formal prayers, too, have their place in the characters' lives. Mary Keane says the Rosary, which combines the tradition of patterned, repetitive prayer with the use of an object of veneration, the beads on which the prayers are counted. Most of the Rosary is made up of Hail Marys, in which Jesus's mother is called upon as one might call upon another woman for assistance, a prayer of petition especially appropriate in moments of need. When Mary Keane's water breaks and she is home alone, she "began a Hail Mary . . . praying all the while the formal prayer that held off both hope and dread" (*AT* 60), chiding herself for not "counting . . . off" the number of Hail Mary she says, as if the efficacy of prayer depended on mathematical precision. Clare, as a sexually active teen, goes to confession, and having confessed allowing Gregory to "take some liberties," is given "for her penance four Our Father's and four Hail Mary's and the avoidance of the 'occasion of sin'" (*AT* 265), the latter being an opportunity for repeating the offense (*AT* 265). Having repeated the offense anyway, the pregnant Clare seems to confuse spirituality with magic, as she prays for the impossible, to stop time so that her pregnancy will not become visible.

Imitatio Mariae: Moral Applications

McDermott's characters retain the habit of prayer even if their relationship with the institutional Church has long faded. Mary Keane's son Michael experiences an oddly timed memory that testifies not only to the durability but also to the spiritual power of the prayers learned in childhood. In the midst of a casual sexual encounter, Michael remembers most of the same prayer that provides the novel's title: "Hail, Holy Queen, Mother of Mercy. Our life, our sweetness and our hope. . . . To thee do we cry, poor banished children of Eve, to thee do we send up our sighs, mourning and weeping in this valley of tears. Turn then, most gracious advocate, thine eyes of mercy toward us, and after this our exile show unto us the blessed fruit of thy womb" (*AT* 186). As the prayer indicates, the role of Mary in the Christian life is as a source of mercy and hope. She stands in opposition to Eve, whose "banishment" from Eden was punishment for sin. The children of Eve—all humanity, likewise banished—can appeal to Mary to "advocate" for them with God, much as a kind mother would present a child's case to a stern, authoritarian father. Life is an "exile" from union with Jesus, and at the end of that earthly exile, Mary is petitioned to facilitate a union with her son. Michael, pre- and/or postcoital, remembers this prayer almost in its entirety, omitting only, but significantly, the next word after "thy womb"—"Jesus." To Michael, the words of the *Salve Regina* are "words you could dismiss as a joke as readily as you could claim them as the precise illustration of everything you wanted" (*AT* 186): a foolish hope, or the promise of an eternally loving mother to care for you here, and hereafter. Thus, Michael engages in the spiritual practice of meditation even as he thought he had "disentangled" himself from the Church.[4]

Mary is a role model for Catholic women, all the more so for Mary Keane in that she is named for the Virgin. Sometimes Mary Keane is successful in her imitation of Mary, as, for example, in the storm scene. Concerned about whether John should have told the children his frightening war story about the death of the first Jacob, she says nothing but instead "considered the wisdom of the Blessed Mother who, as the Christmas gospel told it, pondered everything in her heart" (*AT* 56). A bit of practical marital wisdom, that: a wife does not have to control what her husband says to their children but can keep her thoughts to herself, emulating Jesus's mother in her quiet pondering. But Mary Keane's harsh and judgmental reaction to Clare's announcement of her pregnancy is not consonant with Marian devotion. Mary does not identify Clare with the young, unmarried Mother of Jesus and does not recognize how easily her daughter could have aborted this pregnancy as Susan Persichetti did—or how heroic Clare is not to do so. While Clare is still recovering from her mother's slap on the face, it is Pauline who, wordlessly, simply by allowing Clare to hold her hand, returns the love and acceptance that the girl has always given her. In this one situation, Pauline the virgin undertakes the mothering function briefly abandoned by Mary. The novel began with Mary leaving a church and ends with Clare about to enter a church, as two generations of women begin their lives as wives and mothers, neither aware at that moment of all the joys and sorrows inherent in the role.[5]

The focus here has been on the maternal image in the novel, but it must also be noted that *After This* depicts kind and good men as well: John Keane, protective father and contemplator of eternal verities; Jacob, the lost boy; Michael, lost in his own way; even Gregory, the accidental father who wins his own father's grudging respect by accepting the paternal role. All these are sharply drawn and absorbing characters, as are the women who are not mothers: Susan Persichetti, Professor Wallace, Pauline, and Annie. McDermott's focus in this novel, however, is on living in the female body, especially the fertile female body.

McDermott's next novel is in many ways a parallel to this one much as *At Weddings and Wakes* aligns with *Charming Billy* in their emphasis on the Irish American Catholics of New York City's outer boroughs. Returning to the first-person narrative viewpoint of *That Night* and *Child of My Heart, Someone* consists of the memories of a woman whose life, seen from the outside, is much like Mary Keane's. In a 2017 interview, McDermott recalls how, during the summer of 1992, she felt stalled in her writing career and was seriously considering abandoning it for law school. At a local bar in East Hampton that she and her husband frequented, "Chris, the bar's piano player, sang 'Memory' [from the musical "Cats"] at least once every set."[6] The song, she realized later, inspired her to persevere. Equally important, the song provided her with a continuing focal point for her writing. In *Someone,* McDermott once again returns to the theme of memory, particularly memory as triggered by sensory experience.

CHAPTER 8

Someone (2013)

In *Someone,* Marie Commeford, the first-person narrator, is an old woman in a nursing home looking back on her long and ordinary life. As in *At Weddings and Wakes* and *Charming Billy,* the novel's principle of organization is memory. In *Someone,* the specific focus is on memories formed by strong sensory impressions. A scene crucial to illustrating the nexus between sense and memory is the one in which Marie, in danger of death after a difficult childbirth, receives the last rites of the Catholic Church. This ceremony, then known as extreme unction or last anointing, now known as the sacrament of the anointing of the sick, involves the application of holy oils by a priest on the five points of the body associated with the five senses, asking forgiveness for sins committed through the use of those senses. Sensory imagery in the novel is connected with sin, in keeping with this Catholic tradition, but also and even more emphatically with remembrance. What novelist Leah Hager Cohen, in her review of the novel, calls Marie's "slide show" of memories includes images each of the senses, from smell, taste, touch, hearing, and vision, all of which are connected to specific characters and to key events in Marie's life.[1] Most important, because Marie has been afflicted since childhood with vision problems, are memories related to sight. Visual imagery is associated with distorted and damaged eyesight, with incomplete psychological insight, and, as the reader has come to expect in McDermott's fiction, with the significance of things unseen.

Close Contact: Scent, Touch, Taste

Marie's lifelong vision problems result in compensatory hyperdevelopment of her other senses. In her role as "consoling angel" at Fagin's funeral home (*S* 106), she devises an ingenious way of identifying mourners' coats not by sight, as both she and her employer believe that removing her eyeglasses improves her appearance, but by scent. From childhood, she has associated odors with various environments large and small, with particular objects, and especially with particular people. On the simplest level, ambient scents constitute descriptive elements of settings. An apartment building has its own peculiar aroma, its "fragrant vestibule—fragrant with the onion odor of cooked dinners and the brownstone scent of old wood" (*S* 10), and a candy store is described by its "mingling odors of coffee and newsprint and stale milk" (*S* 82). The Brooklyn of her childhood and young adulthood smells of "car exhaust and heated asphalt, of garbage and incinerator fires" (*S* 50) and "industrial smoke" (*S* 80), while the Long Island town in which she and her husband raise their family features "the suburban smell of cut grass and honeysuckle" (*S* 219). Objects are associated with certain aromas as well and link scenes to each other. Her childhood memories of the fragrance of sheets hung out to dry on a clothesline so that they "retained their odor of sunshine" (*S* 20) are associated with the hotel sheets of her wedding night, which "smelled faintly of bleach and now of our own sleep-warmed bodies" (*S* 173). The combination of these two pleasant images bodes well for her marriage, but another association will be added to the smell of bleach: the hospital sheets during her traumatic first labor.

Sensory imagery preserved in memory also functions as a means of developing characterization. Marie's relationships with men are influenced by her father's drinking habits. Because, during her Prohibition-era childhood, her father would take her to the speakeasy after dinner, she associates the smell of alcohol with her father and thus with men in general. As a child, she does not understand the potential downside of the alluring aroma and her father's obvious efforts to cover up his drinking via pungent aromas, "faded cologne" (*S* 10) and "bay rum" (*S* 64), and as a child, Marie does not associate his drinking with the smell of his vomit. Because of Marie's love for her father, the smell of alcohol is a defining attribute of manliness: she is attracted to a "man in a suit" at Dora Ryan's false wedding because of "the unmistakable smell of drink on his breath, a lovely, masculine scent, I thought, because it was my father's" (*S* 34).

Given this association between men and the smell of alcohol, it is not surprising that she almost marries an alcoholic. Walter Hartnett is at first attractive to Marie at least partially because he smells and tastes of beer. Years later, when he reappears at Fagin's funeral home for Bill Corrigan's wake, his scent calls up the memory not only of her early sexual foreplay with Walter but also of her father: "The odor of cigarettes and alcohol seemed to be woven into the fabric of his suit. It was a charm to me still, alcohol on a man's breath"

(*S* 141). More mature at that point, Marie understands that that smell, along with a glimpse of a flask in his pocket, are danger signs. Unlike Walter, the man Marie marries, Tom Commeford, is associated with positive scents. On their wedding night he smells of champagne, but just enough to pass Marie's litmus test for male attractiveness. Tom is also associated with domestic, nurturing aromas. To prepare for her long-delayed homecoming with their first baby, Tom cleans their apartment and prepares food: "all was Spic and Span and lemon polish and the lingering odor of the apple pie Tom had taught himself to bake that morning" (*S* 191). The combination of these scents indicate that Tom is the perfect man for Marie: a suggestion of her lost father, without her father's tendency to excess, and with a capacity for nurturing.

Tom and Walter are also compared to her father and contrasted with each other via the sensations involved in permissible and impermissible touch. Marie remembers how, when she and her father would walk to the speakeasy after dinner, he would tell her to wait outside, pressing her shoulders as if to set her more firmly on the ground. While bringing a child along on such an errand might be questionable, the physical contact is acceptable, loving, a positive memory for Marie. Marie's first experience of foreplay, with Walter, is crude, abrupt, and painful, indicative of his presumptuous attitude toward her body. A sexual novice, Marie does not understand that Walter has transgressed. In contrast, on their wedding night, Tom politely asks for permission—"If I may" (*S* 170)—before he approaches his new wife. Even the doctor who delivers Marie's first child, as savage in his way as was Walter in his, partially redeems himself by asking permission to touch. Before checking her incision, he asks permission, echoing Tom's kindness on their wedding night—"If I may" (*S* 183)—and Marie appreciates this "polite caution" (*S* 183), however belated.

Marie's role as a housewife and mother is affected by remembered aromas associated with food preparation. A formative experience for Marie is her brief acquaintance with Gerty Hanson's mother, a woman Marie associates with food and cooking. "Mrs. Hanson smelled of wholesome things, sunshine and oatmeal and yeast" (*S* 31), and their whole apartment has "good smells" (*S* 32); everything about Mrs. Hanson makes her an archetypal mother figure. When Mrs. Hanson dies in childbirth, cooking is poisoned for Marie because she associates learning to cook with taking over a mother's role in the household, as Gerty does after her mother dies. This accounts for an otherwise confusing episode in which Marie resists, and finally sabotages, learning to bake soda bread. She and her mother bicker over the steps involved in its preparation. Once the bread is in the oven, Marie is left alone to supervise it because her mother has to go to "the city," a trip Marie connects with her father's illness. Marie's mother seems not to be psychologically astute and cannot understand that the subtext of Marie's refusal to cook is anxiety over the threatened loss of a parent. This aversion to cooking continues into her married life, and so Tom Commeford—adaptability being another of his husbandly virtues—learns to bake an apple pie.

Years later, her children grown and the two boys no longer living regularly at home, Marie has still not improved as a cook. At her brother Gabe's homecoming, surely a special occasion, Marie serves an uninspired meal consisting of "sliced ham and coleslaw from the deli, cucumbers in vinegar, potato salad, and bakery rolls" (*S* 214). Although she describes herself as "making dinner" (*S* 214), this process might better be described as "unwrapping dinner." But the roots of her fear of cooking for a family were set long ago in the Hansons' kitchen. Forever after, Marie associates certain cooking smells, like that of the vinegar in which the deli soaks the cucumbers, with death. The smell of vinegar calls up a complex group of memories, all of them sad: the embalming rooms in the funeral home; the hospital when she is sick after childbirth; and, "when they read that part of the Passion where Jesus said, I thirst, and a sponge soaked with wine and vinegar was raised to his lips" (*S* 39), the agonizing death of Jesus. Although Gerty Hanson has taught Marie that vinegar can be used to boil eggs properly for dyeing at Eastertime to celebrate Jesus' resurrection, to Marie its odor only means death.

Overheard: Repetition and Memory

Words and phrases heard in childhood—repeated by her parents, remembered for a lifetime—become part of Marie's definition of herself. Her parents call her "a bold piece" (*S* 57), apparently intending the phrase as a criticism tinged with humor and a perverse pride. Repetition of the phrase links several disparate scenes taking place over long intervals of time. During the soda bread episode, having opinions of her own about cooking makes her, in her mother's eyes, a "bold piece" (*S* 57), a rebellious child, for not meekly conforming to her womanly role in the kitchen. Speaking up to an ophthalmologist, less deferential to the medical profession than she was during her first childbirth, causes her to think of herself approvingly as an assertive woman, a "bold piece" (*S* 94). The most significant use of the phrase occurs when she resumes sexual relations with Tom after the difficult birth of her first child. Although the brutal doctor has advised against her having another child, she initiates sexual activity with Tom immediately upon her return home. She is proud of herself. She has not only survived childbirth but triumphed: "I was a bold piece. I had stood at death's door. I had withstood pain. I knew I could make a stand against it, against time, bold and stubborn, a living child in my arms" (*S* 193). At this point she embraces the term as a mark of honor. Years later, in the nursing home, she remembers the phrase and recounts the episode to her caregiver. At this point the phrase is a way of asserting her identity in the face of old age and imminent death.

Marie's parents often use another key term to describe her, "little pagan," to stress what they perceive as the stark contrast between her and her brother. Marie sees this as their way of evaluating her as the lesser of the two siblings. Normal childhood behavior, to Marie's parents, seem an indication of the child's lack of Christian virtue, which the mother seems to take seriously, the father less so. Thinking of her daughter (unfairly) as prone to pagan behavior causes Marie's mother to punish the child for using the Irish term *amadan* without considering whether a child that age could understand its negative connotations. When Marie's parents recall the incident, it is in a quasi-humorous way: "They called me 'our little pagan' after that, whenever their pride in my brother's saintliness was in need of some deflating" (*S* 26). But Marie, then and in memory, registers the phrase as indicating the clear preference that the parents had for their son. They define their daughter by contrast to Gabe, who seems at that point destined to be a priest, perhaps even a bishop. This pattern of thinking becomes part of Marie's sense of herself and even permeates her attitude toward her own daughters, whom she regards as "little pagans" also. While Marie eventually embraces the term "bold piece" and redefines it as an honorific, she continues even in adulthood to imagine herself as less than Gabe, their parents' "golden child" (*S* 226). Repeated phrases such as these, engraved in memory even if not supported by evidence, shape Marie's sense of herself.

Sight, Hindsight, Insight

"Men don't make passes at girls who wear glasses." At the time Marie is growing up, this commonplace seemed true, even to women. Walter Hartnett, her first boyfriend, denigrates her appearance both with glasses and without. She describes her own eyes as "offending," "scrinching" (*S* 66), showing that she has internalized Walter's attitude. What Marie is doing with her glasses at any given point in the novel is an expression of both conscious and unconscious reactions. Marie takes off and puts on her glasses, often misplaces them, and in the course of all this fidgeting impairing her own physical vision but also her perceptions and judgments, sometimes even deliberately. This is most significant in the scene in which Walter breaks up with her. Because she is hyperattentive to visual cues, she has noticed that Walter never looks straight at her, his "veering attention" (*S* 67) signaling detachment. Meeting him at a restaurant for what she expects will be a pleasant date, she takes off her glasses, wanting to appear more attractive to him, even though this means she can only see him vaguely, "the shape of him" (*S* 77), not details. Thus, is she literally blindsided by the breakup. On the verge of ending their relationship, he tells her to put the glasses back on again so she will be more recognizable to him. Then, egregiously, he uses her vision defect—"blind you" (*S* 78)—as an excuse to break up with her; "he wants to marry someone who has 'no flaws that he could see.'"[2] Marie carries the emotional scars of this episode for the rest of her life, and when she recounts the narrative, she expresses her understanding of it in visual terms. Years later, she warns her daughters about men like Walter: "If he looks over your head while you're talking, get rid of him" (*S* 66). Ironically, though Walter deems her blind, Marie chooses her life partner more wisely than Walter does.

Marie's poor eyesight is sometimes useful as a protection against what she does not want to see. When she is working at Fagin's funeral parlor, she removes her glasses during wakes for children, allows her vision to blur, and averts her gaze. Poor vision serves her well in these circumstances, as seeing clearly would be devastating. Her inability to confront the truth about her brother Gabe is similarly expressed in terms of distorted sight. In the daytime, with her glasses on, she sees her brother clearly, but she prefers to see him in the dark: "the brother I saw with my glasses on . . . was far less familiar to me than this one of uncertain edges and soft darkness" (*S* 20). That is, concerning her brother, she prefers not knowing to knowing. She "prefers" to see Gabe indistinctly, in her "peripheral vision": "Here he was again as I preferred him . . . the familiar blur of his profile seen through my distorted vision" (*S* 84). The parallel between the two situations involving blurred vision, wakes for children and her brother's mental illness, indicates that she unwittingly uses her poor physical vision to provide emotional protection. Marie is never able to articulate, even in her own mind, that what her daughters and her husband see, that Gabe is gay, is in fact true. Marie also prefers not to see that Gabe's extreme stress is the result of the sexual guilt that is so prevalent among Catholics, especially Irish Catholics. Gabe's lost vocation and lonely life thereafter is a direct result of the sense of sin imposed upon him by their Church. Marie thinks she sees "the clear-eyed truth of it" (*S* 131), but she does not.

Marie, then, is limited in many ways, of which her weak eyesight is a metaphor. As is the case with many first-person narratives, the reader sees what the narrator does not. With only a basic education and little experience of the world, she accepts Walter Hartnett's edict that she should limit her job possibilities to Brooklyn, an acceptance that even outlasts her relationship with Walter, and she never questions her mother's suggestion that she answer a want ad for "typists or switchboard operators" (*S* 97). She is unaware of the effects on her of such factors as her parents' preferential treatment of her brother, the loss of significant people in her childhood, the continuing pain of Walter Hartnett's rejection, and the reasons behind her brother's abandonment of the priesthood. She has neither career ambitions, intellectual interests, nor psychological acuity. Trained in subordination and self-effacement, she does not give herself credit for the qualities she does have: for her courage in facing the pain of childbirth three more times after her traumatic first experience, for her wisdom in choosing Tom, for her generosity of spirit in accepting Gabe, for her loyalty to family and to faith.

Visionary Experience: The Spirituality of Sight

Marie's vocabulary of vision draws on the scriptural analogy between physical sight and spiritual insight, and, conversely, physical and spiritual blindness and darkness. *Someone* is unique in Alice McDermott's body of work thus far in its meditation on a pre-life as well as an afterlife. No tradition guides Marie in her thinking about "that other, earlier uncertainty: the darkness before the slow coming to awareness of the first light" (*S* 10), only her own personal associations with imagery of sight and blindness. Marie wonders why there is not more theological examination of this issue, why "all the faith and all the fancy, all the fear, the speculation, all the wild imaginings that go into the study of heaven and hell" (*S* 10) have concentrated on life after death rather than before conception. None of the key terms of Marie's meditation on the afterlife suggest the kind of unquestioning faith that one might expect from a committed Christian. There is only "uncertainty," "fancy," "speculation," "wild imaginings," "darkness." St. Paul's definition of faith is "evidence of things not seen" (Hebrews 11:1). That paradoxical definition is related to blind Bill Corrigan's "second sight" (*S* 136), his preternatural capacity to umpire sporting events; to the hallucinatory visions Marie sees in her old age, "figures appearing here and there, mostly in my peripheral vision" (*S* 176); and to the Catholic faith that Marie shares with her husband and brother.

Another similar pattern of imagery has to do with reflections rather than direct sight: in water, in a looking glass, through glass, through tears. Marie sees herself, her mother, her father, and Pegeen Chehab reflected in mirrors or panes of glass; she sees Gerty Hansen from a window, hopes to see the disappointed Dora Ryan at a window, and sees her father for the last time at a window, "waving to us from behind the sky's reflection" (*S* 64). After Gabe leaves the priesthood, Marie sees the ordinary world through two sets of transparencies, "the tears that were trapped under my glasses washing up over my eyes" (*S* 78). These references call to mind the passage from St. Paul's first letter to the Corinthians: "For now we see through a glass, darkly, but then face to face:

now I know in part; but then shall I know even as also I am known" (13:12). The things of this world, the sensory world, are mere reflections of a higher reality, "the ordinary days . . . a veil, a swath of thin cloth that distorted the eye" (*S* 80).

Tom Commeford's meditation on the biblical images of sight and blindness is based on his memory of a sermon Gabe once preached. The situation leading into Tom Commeford's discussion is that Marie and Tom have run into each other at a party and renewed their acquaintance. Tom walks Marie home, and she invites him upstairs to visit with Gabe, who Tom knew as a priest. The conversation leads to Tom's telling his war stories about how he and his fellow soldiers would make art supplies from spit and clay, which in turn reminds Tom of Gabe's sermon. Gabe was preaching on a passage from John's gospel:

> And as he was passing by, he saw a man blind from birth. And his disciples asked him, "Rabbi, who has sinned, this man or his parents, that he should be born blind?" Jesus answered, "Neither has this man sinned, nor his parents, but the works of God were to be made manifest in him. I must do the works of him who sent me while it is day; night is coming, when no one can work. As long as I am in the world I am the light of the world." (John 9: 1–5)

Jesus explains that the healing of the blind man is not so much a physical matter as it is a way of demonstrating the spiritual significance of the sense of sight and the power of light. That said, Jesus mixes clay with his own spittle, applies it to the blind man's eyes as if medicinally, and the blind man sees.

The tactile images of the clay and the spittle are characteristically vivid examples of the literary style of the Gospels, so it is natural that they remain in Tom's memory as related to his war experience involving those same substances. What impressed Tom at the time of Gabe's sermon was Gabe's comment that this is the only incident when Jesus healed someone "without being asked . . . Without a profession of faith" (*S* 162). This, said Tom, reassured him during the war: "It was a good thing to remember, over there. That you didn't necessarily have to ask. Or even believe. It gave me hope" (*S* 163). Tom gained spiritual benefits from this sermon; therefore, Gabe was, and still is, a good priest, bringing his small congregation closer to Jesus. How blind is the Church to drive away such as he.

Tom's declaration of hope rather than faith is a characteristic element of the varieties of religious experience found in McDermott's novels. Faith is belief in that which is imperceptible by the senses, but because the senses are the connection between the self and the world, belief is difficult, even impossible, without hope. Another important set of images, those associated with falling, are relevant here. Physical falls are reminders of the biblical Fall from grace into sin, and the hope nevertheless that there is "Someone beyond our expectations who catches and sustains us."[3] There is no certainty, however: Tom Commeford survives his fall from the airplane; Marie falls but is caught by her caregiver; but Pegeen Chehab's handsome stranger does not arrive to catch her when she falls.[4] Faith is not certainty, and often wavers. Better, then, to rely on hope.

At this point in the examination of Alice McDermott's body of work, it is increasingly obvious that the novelist develops central themes throughout her work but also that variants of lightly developed characters in one novel return to be more fully developed in another. In *Someone,* for example, Big Lucy and her mother, the latter recognizable for her enormous goiter as well as her furious loyalty to her damaged daughter, and even Walter Hartnett and his limp all foreshadow the physical and moral grotesques of *The Ninth Hour.* This her most recent novel has been published to outstanding reviews. At a lecture at her alma mater, Sacred Heart Academy, McDermott noted that this, of all her novels, shocked her husband, presumably because of something in it that was different from the others.[5] While the novel recapitulates many of the characteristic themes of her earlier novels, it also contains increased attention to damaged bodies and broken spirits.

CHAPTER 9

The Ninth Hour (2017)

In *The Ninth Hour* McDermott returns to the world of Irish American Catholic Brooklyn, the setting for *At Weddings and Wakes* and *Someone*, and the mid-twentieth-century time frame of all her novels thus far. In this world, the complexities of practicing the Catholic faith involve applying theological principles to pastoral practice. What is, and should be, the Church's protocol for the burial of suicides? What, if any, authority do religious sisters have in adapting Church policy to individual circumstances? Does the virtuous Catholic life require asceticism? And all of these relate to the "big, universal questions"[1]: is there an afterlife, and if there is, who or what determines the fate of the individual soul therein? All these issues are explored via the memories of a collective narrator, the younger generation of the family begun in early-twentieth-century New York by a young Irish emigrant couple, Annie and Jim, "'Mc-something,'" as a police officer calls them, "'of Irish extraction'" (NH 11).

Irish American Catholics in the Outer Boroughs

The Brooklynites of *The Ninth Hour* have limited education, lower-middle-class social status, and blue-collar careers. Annie, the protagonist's mother, is a laundry worker in a convent; her husband, Jim, was a motorman for the transit system. Sally, the protagonist, has a high school education, and the apex of her career, before she marries Patrick Tierney, a laborer, is a part-time job as a waitress. The Tierneys, Patrick's parents, are similarly situated, economically and socially. Michael Tierney is a doorman, and his wife, Liz, before marriage, was a domestic. They associate mainly with each other and with the Catholic sisters of the parish.

Like the characters in *After This*, the characters in *The Ninth Hour* speak Catholic as their first language. They think in the vocabulary of formal prayers, hymns, and scriptural references. Even as he makes final preparations for his suicide, Jim says the "Hail Mary," asking for the Virgin's help "*Now and at the hour of our death*" (*NH* 6; italics McDermott's). The view of this earthly life as being a "vale of tears" (*NH* 13) is similarly taken from the *Salve Regina,* the prayer to the Virgin Mary that features so prominently in *After This.* The nuns mark time not only according to the liturgical year, as do all Catholics, but also according to the canonical hours in "The Horarium" (*NH* 48), a daily schedule of formal prayers. As novelist Mary Gordon points out in her review of the novel, the ninth hour is "the time for prayer that occurs at 3 in the afternoon," traditionally regarded as "the hour that Jesus died," but also, oddly, the time of "the less spiritual encounters Annie regularly indulges at the very same time."[2] The auditory environment of the nuns' world includes "the sound of the morning psalm [that] floated from the chapel" (*NH* 64) and the traditional Latin hymn "*O Salutaris Hostia*" (*NH* 65). In addition to the formal liturgy of the Church year, the Catholic school year includes such observances as vocation days, semicomic events in which "the students were asked to dress up as priests and nuns and to parade about the schoolyard as miniature ecclesiastics" (*NH* 79) for the purpose of clerical recruitment.

Catholic character types also include not only the clergy but laypeople like the Tierneys, who represent the ideals of Catholic marriage as understood at the time. Michael Tierney is for most of the novel a shadowy figure who works hard to support his ever-growing brood. But he had already achieved a kind of nobility in his youth when he rejected his father's materialistic and social-climbing aspirations for him and married Liz, an Irish emigrant and a domestic servant, at the cost of losing his inheritance and his relationship with his father. Liz Tierney, joyfully procreative, loving the "chaos, busyness, bustling" of her six-child household (*NH* 215), is "a devout Catholic, but the kind of Catholic . . . who preferred the noise and humidity of the street after mass to the cool dampness of the sacristy, preferred conversation to prayer, sunlight to flickering shadow" (*NH* 215). When she falls asleep beside her husband and with "maybe a child or two snagged in the covers" before her evening prayers are done, she does so before reaching the sorrowful part of the "Hail Mary": "*Now and at the hour of our death*" (*NH* 215; italics McDermott's). Literally as well as figuratively full of life due to her repeated pregnancies, she serves as a foil to the dreary Mrs. Costello. Sister Lucy introduces Annie to Liz with the intention of supplying a support system for the widowed mother. Thereafter, Liz stands by her friend unquestioningly and without regard to moral orthodoxy, accepting Annie's relationship with Mr. Costello and welcoming Sally into her already crowded home when Annie refuses to take Sally back after the girl's failed trip to the novitiate.

Compared to the Tierneys and to the nuns, priests do not come off too well in this novel. One claims credit for work a nun did; another has his eye on the convent property and would just as soon get the nuns out. Although the priests, like the nuns, are "allowed to be human . . . both flawed and graced," as Ann Thurston observes of their counterparts in *After This*,[3] the priests are more flawed than graced. In plot time, the sexual abuse scandal perpetrated by some priests, and condoned and even facilitated by others, is poisoning the Church from within, as the author knows, as readers know, but as the characters do not. Liz's disapproval is based on her perception that the priests are "pampered momma's boys. . . . 'Princes of the Church, my eye,' she would say. . . . 'Spoiled children they are. It's the nuns who keep things running'" (*NH* 214). The many things that the nuns keep running include, in one case literally, the affairs of the laity.

The nuns seem cloistered, but from their vantage points in the convent and around the neighborhood, they see what people need and try to meet those needs via a "compassionate and professional form of social welfare."[4] This sometimes puts them at odds with ecclesiastical officialdom. At the time in which the novel is set, suicides were not permitted to be buried with full religious rites or in hallowed ground. By concealing Jim's cause of death, Sister St. Saviour tries, but fails, to get Jim buried in Calvary, a vast Catholic cemetery in Woodside, Queens, where Annie and Jim already own a burial plot. In two cases, Sister Lucy serves as a manager of relationships between lay women and even between those women and their men. Sister Lucy, defined by her ability to "insist," arranges for Annie to become friends with Liz Tierney. More surprisingly, Sister Lucy notices an attraction between Annie and the married Mr. Costello and comes to the unorthodox conclusion that Annie needs a "proper husband" (*NH* 57) to replace Jim—never mind that said husband is already married to another woman. So Sister Lucy arranges for Annie to have a respite from laundry duties and child care during the day, ostensibly to "catch her breath" and "go to stores," but actually to have sex—that is, in Catholic terms, time off to commit adultery. Sister Lucy is not unique in her sensitivity to the sexual needs of a young woman like Annie; Sister Illuminata, the chief laundress, also understands that "hunger" between men and women (*NH* 195). When the couple's affair can no longer be ignored, Sister Lucy advocates for Annie to stay in her job at the convent laundry, even if Annie refuses to end the affair, that is, again in Catholic terms, to avoid the occasions of sin. When Annie prioritizes her relationship with her milkman and refuses to accept Sally back into her childhood home after her abortive trip to the convent, Sister Lucy does not attempt to dissuade Annie from her choice of Mr. Costello over her daughter but instead arranges for Sally to live with the Tierneys. Except for the housing arrangement for Sally, none of these decisions would pass theological muster; the nuns "interpret Catholic theology and local ethics flexibly. Maybe even lawlessly."[5]

While the sisters appear to accept "the rigidity of the Catholic world view," they "maneuver within that framework" in accordance with their own code of ethics.[6] In addition to their penchant for aiding and abetting adultery, they quietly rebel against the policies of their Church and even of their religious order. Like Liz, they are no fans of the priests, which is another implicit critique of the Church's male hierarchy. In their nonconfrontational way, they undermine clerical authority by evading Church rules and customs in big ways and small, such as when Sister Illuminata talks about her past in "the world," despite the rules of her order, or when Sister St. Saviour wants Jim "buried in Calvary because the power of the Church wanted him kept out and she, who had spent her life in the Church's service, wanted him in" (*NH* 30). Sister St. Saviour protests that "it would be a different Church if I were running it" (*NH* 63), but since she and her fellow nuns never directly confront the power structure of the Church, never attempt to run it, their quiet rebellion leads nowhere. The nuns' complicity in this domination of female religious orders by male clergy is suggested by the fact that several of the religious orders named in the pseudo-litany have "little" in their names, with its connotation of childlike submissiveness. While accepting what appears to be a low position in the ecclesiastical pecking order, these nuns actually constitute "a community of female superheroes" in the world of needy Brooklynites.[7]

Of the different ways in which the sisters in this novel diverge from the stereotype, none is more significant than in their special attachment to Sally. This too is against both the spirit and the letter of their commitment to their religious order. These childless women are, ideally, supposed to sublimate the love they might have had for a child of their own into love of God. It is clear to the reader if not to the nuns themselves that their love for Sally is for Sally herself, not particularly for the divinity as reflected in Sally. The nuns act as supplementary mothers to Sally ostensibly as an act of charity but in reality to fulfill their own frustrated maternal longings. Sister Illuminata is quite conscious that she vies for Sally's affections not with Annie, her biological mother, but with Sister Jeanne: "It was sinful, the way she competed with Jeanne. . . . Her need to be the girl's favorite, to be loved beyond all other nuns in the convent by this confused and mortal child, was inexplicable, even to herself. A hunger" (*NH* 191). This rivalry will affect the behavior of Sister Jeanne in the climactic scene, the death of Mrs. Costello.

That scene illustrates how life in a Catholic world promotes a specific way of thinking. The characters have never seriously considered any alternative thought systems; they think inside the Catholic box, occasionally disagreeing with the Church's position on a given issue, but never failing to take that position into account. The effort to formulate their own ideas while not running too dramatically afoul of doctrine leads to some convoluted logic regarding important ethical and theological issues.

Moral Acrobatics: The Death of Mrs. Costello

Casuistry is a branch of moral theology that applies general principles to specific cases via logical reasoning; the term also has acquired the connotation of using convoluted logic to evade those principles. The moral decisions made by various characters in the novel illustrate both kinds of casuistry. Sister St. Saviour, for example, applies casuistical reasoning in both senses of the term to circumvent the Church's rules on the burial of suicides in Jim's case, and all the nuns make many exceptions to the Church's strict norms of sexual morality in Annie and Mr. Costello's case. In the first example, the prohibition regarding the burial of suicides in Catholic cemeteries, Sister St. Saviour unknowingly anticipates the direction in which pastoral practices will evolve with greater understanding of mental illness,[8] but she attempts to evade the rules in place at the time. In the second case, that of Annie and her milkman, the Church's prohibition of adultery stands, and the nuns never question it, but they condone the relationship and even facilitate it. In both of these examples, the novel exemplifies what, seventeen years before the publication of *The Ninth Hour,* McDermott called the "moral and physical acrobatics performed in order to maintain and defy the letter of church law."[9] All of the nuns have shown themselves capable of these "acrobatics." Two of them, Sister Jeanne and Sister Lucy, play a far more serious role in a third case: speeding the passing of Mrs. Costello. The general principle could not be clearer: "Thou shalt not kill." On this principle, the Catholic Church forbids euthanasia. But in the case of Mrs. Costello, it seems that the Catholic women who surround her, even the nuns, are willing to make an exception in her case. And, using their own brand of logic, they find what seem to them valid theological justifications.

Sally's reasoning is as follows. Nun *manqué,* she fears for the salvation of her adulterous mother's soul, all the more because she believes that her mother will never amend her life as the sacrament of penance requires. Therefore, the only hope for her mother is to marry Mr. Costello. Divorce is not possible for Catholics and annulments infrequent and difficult to obtain. So Mrs. Costello's continued existence is a barrier to that marriage and a danger to Annie's immortal soul. Thus it follows, according to Sally's reasoning, that Mrs. Costello needs to die. Via this sophistical chain of reasoning, and adrift because of the failure of her plans to enter the novitiate, Sally becomes convinced that killing

Mrs. Costello is not only "something she might actually accomplish in this world" but an act of moral heroism, rendering "her mother's life, her mortal life and her eternal life, restored" (*NH* 224). Murder is a mortal sin, but for the murderer only, not for anyone who unknowingly benefited from the murder. By condemning her own soul to eternal damnation, Sally believes that she can save the soul of her mother. Ironically, working exclusively with Catholic concepts leads Sally to a most non-Christian conclusion: murder compensates for her failure to become a nun.

Sister Jeanne's thought processes are similarly complex and similarly casuistical in the pejorative sense of the term. In the novitiate, Sister Jeanne must have studied theology and therefore should know better, but she too engages in ideological gymnastics. Sister Jeanne appears to know that Sally is attempting to poison Mrs. Costello by feeding her tea mixed with alum. Because of her love for Sally and her rivalry with Sister Illuminata, Jeanne decides to kill Mrs. Costello herself before Sally can do it, thus preventing Sally from committing a sin. This accounts for Sally's memory of the scene of Mrs. Costello's death. At the bedside of the invalid, "Sally recalled the way Sister Jeanne had put out her arm as she'd tried to near Mrs. Costello's bed, blocking her way" (*NH* 230). Sister Jeanne is preventing Sally from killing Mrs. Costello by doing it herself. The nun may have even devised a plan for a perfect crime in that she feeds Mrs. Costello in such a way that she will likely develop aspiration pneumonia, a common threat to the elderly and infirm. Sister Aquina has warned against feeding Mrs. Costello chunky applesauce containing peels, and nursing sisters should know this even without warning. When Sister Jeanne does just that, applesauce is weaponized.

When the inevitable crisis occurs, Sister Lucy's response to the call for help is similarly ambiguous. Sister Lucy has been skeptical heretofore about the reality of Mrs. Costello's invalidism, regarding her complaints as the histrionics of a faker. When Sister Lucy embraces Mrs. Costello, it is unclear whether she is attempting to comfort her or to suppress her breathing. On top of all this, earlier in the novel it is stated that "rheumatic fever as a child had left her [Mrs. Costello] with a weak heart" (*NH* 58). If this were a crime novel, it would not be clear what killed Mrs. Costello. But regarding Catholic beliefs on euthanasia, it is clear that both Sally and Sister Jeanne, perhaps even Sister Lucy, are culpable because of their intention. They planned to end the life of Mrs. Costello, and no virtuous end can justify these means.

It is noteworthy that none of these cradle Catholics, whether nuns or laywomen, consider going to confession. Sincere repentance, expressed in confession to a priest, would allow them to be forgiven for their sins. But they never seem to think of this possibility or of availing themselves of pastoral counseling outside confession. This might be yet another implicit condemnation of the clergy in the mid-twentieth-century Church: even before the abuse scandals were public knowledge, the priests seem peripheral figures, pretentious but ineffectual. So both Sister Jeanne and Sally make up their own minds about theological matters, and not necessarily in a way that might allow them to forgive themselves. At the end of her life, Sister Jeanne thinks that she has committed the unforgivable sin, a concept well-known in, but actually incompatible with, Catholicism in that it negates the belief in God's infinite mercy. Sister Jeanne does not want forgiveness because, by her reasoning, murdering Mrs. Costello and going to hell in Sally's place is the ultimate proof of her love for Sally, a love greater than that of her rivals, Annie and Sister Illuminata. Sally has her own strange theory of eternal punishment, believing that she could bring her mother to heaven by damning herself to hell. Both have reasoned their way to the theologically dubious conclusions that adultery is so serious a sin that it justifies murder, and that volunteering for eternal damnation is the ultimate act of love.

Damaged Bodies, Damned Souls

An unprecedented emphasis on the damaged, distorted, mutilated, suffering body distinguishes *The Ninth Hour* from most of McDermott's previous novels but is suggested by its immediate predecessor, *Someone*. Blind Bill Corrigan's war wound and Marie's defective eyes are recurrent images in that novel. The grotesque body appears there in the person of Big Lucy, whose unattractive appearance, developmental problems, and perseverations on sexual topics foreshadow the woman on the train in *The Ninth Hour.* The damaged body recurs in the descriptions of Mrs. Costello and of the mothers of Sister Illuminata and Sister Lucy. The condition of the human body after death, introduced in the scenes in the funeral home in *Someone,* is an important topic in this novel. Unlike earlier novels, *The Ninth Hour* also forges a connection between the distorted human body and diseases of the spirit.

Red Whelan, "The Substitute," is a prime example of the grotesque. His tale, part of the Tierney family legacy, is told by Michael Tierney to his son, Patrick. During the Civil War, as was legal at the time, Red Whelan was hired as a substitute for Michael's father, Patrick's grandfather. Thus, according to family lore as recounted to Michael, all the family's later success is attributable to Red Whelan, "the man who served in the Union Army so my father didn't have to. . . . Made it possible for me to be born" (*NH* 170), and by extension the younger generation, including Patrick. So it comes to pass that when Whelan returns from the war horribly mutilated, with "scarred red flesh from neck to ear as if a plow had scraped his face. One leg and one arm" (*NH* 71), he spends the rest of his life at the Tierney house in the care of the elder Patrick's sister Rose, who takes it upon herself to fulfill the family obligation.

The bare facts of Red Whelan's fate are tragic, but tragic also is its effect on Michael's father. For all his long life, the elder Patrick experiences a sense of guilt so overwhelming that he comes to believe that all later actions by all Tierneys must be worthy of Red Whelan's suffering, so he appoints himself arbiter of what actions are or are not worthy. He defines worthiness narrowly, in terms of social status, thus imposing a false standard on his son, which leads in turn to their irreconcilable conflict. The elder Patrick was a socially climbing schoolteacher who took his young son, Michael, to visit a wealthy family summering in Poughkeepsie, where Michael fell in love with the housekeeper, Liz, who would become his wife and the younger Patrick's mother. As Michael tells the tale, his father "didn't want me coming down in the world" (*NH* 168) by marrying a domestic servant, deeming the marriage a violation of the Red Whelan principle: "'Is this what Red Whelan threw away an arm and a leg for?' his father asked him. (Our father, telling us the story, added, 'Thus coining a phrase.') 'So the fruit of his sacrifice can drag us back to the slums?'" (*NH* 176). And Michael replied: "'One life's already been given to save your skin. I won't give you mine as well.' Those were the last words we ever exchanged" (*NH* 176). This father–son relationship is far more damaged than is Red Whelan's body. The measure of Michael's continued love for his father nonetheless is the fact that Michael names his son after the estranged father and takes the younger Patrick with him to the funeral.

The impact of Red Whelan's story is so dramatic that the younger Patrick expects the man himself to be extraordinary, as per his starring role in the family drama. But when Patrick meets the man for the first time at his grandfather's funeral, the boy is disappointed. Whelan is indifferent to his value as a symbol, indifferent to the Tierneys, to the progeny engendered because of his sacrifice: he only wants his lunch. And it is clear to the reader, if not to the young Patrick, that Whelan, though he has surely lost much, has also gained much: a place to live comfortably free of charge and the single-minded devotion of Rose. It becomes clear also that, in service to his perceived obligation to Red Whelan, the elder Patrick has mutilated his own life.

Descent into the Underworld: The Train Ride to Hell

Distorted and damaged bodies also play a part in Sally's changing her mind about joining a religious order—in Catholic terminology, the loss of her vocation. Sally's train ride to the novitiate in Chicago employs the folkloric motif of the descent into a supernatural underworld from which the traveler emerges with an altered view of the natural world. Once above ground again, Sally can no longer accept her original reasons for entering the convent, based as it was on another piece of faulty reasoning, an analogy between convent life and a state of health and cleanliness.

Sally's original attraction to the convent was influenced by Sister Illuminata's explanation of her own vocation as based on a divine call "to become, in a ghastly world, the pure, clean antidote to filth, to pain" (*NH* 89), a "sweet, clean antidote to suffering, to pain" (*NH* 90). The repetition of the word "clean" underlines the fact that this is the reasoning process of a laundress, for whom the analogy between physical cleanliness and moral purity would naturally seem persuasive. This idea appeals to Sally, a girl raised in a laundry. She comes to see her function in the world as analogous to that of the bandages washed in the laundry daily and sent out with the sisters on their visits to the sick. Laundering becomes a spiritual metaphor for the function of the nun in the world, to "transform what is ugly, soiled, stained . . . [and] send it back into the world like a resurrected soul" (*NH* 91).[10] Sister Illuminata reinforces the cleanliness imagery by encouraging Sally to take the name Mary Immaculate as her name in religion. The convent, then, to Sally, is a nexus of healing purity in a diseased and dirty world.

But the train ride so affects her that by the time she reaches Chicago, Sally has lost her vocation. She returns home, "like some Odysseus, much older and much changed" (*NH* 161). The reference is to Book XI of Homer's *Odyssey*, in which Odysseus visits the underworld.[11] Parallels between the chapter entitled "Overnight" and this section of Homer's *Odyssey* are clear and obviously intended. At the direction of Circe, Odysseus digs a pit and "poured libation to all the dead" (l. 25), which causes them, one by one, to appear from below ("They drifted up to the pit from all sides / With an eerie cry" [ll. 40–41]) and tell their stories. First is Elpenor, who had died in Circe's court, still "unmourned, unburied" (l. 50). Then Odysseus' mother, Anticleia, relates to Odysseus the circumstances of her death and reports on the situation regarding Penelope back in Ithaca; then the prophet Tiresias foretells the events of Odysseus's long journey home from Troy. All speak to Odysseus at length. A succession of more briefly characterized speakers follow, "the wives and daughters of the heroes of old" (l. 229), and Odysseus is overwhelmed by their stories. The major elements of the scene incorporated into the parallel chapter in *The Ninth Hour* are the descent into the "pit," the meeting with the dead, the storytelling, and Odysseus' dramatic reaction. McDermott has used the mythic theme of the underground journey to the land of the dead before, in Lucy's repeated trips back to her family's apartment in Brooklyn in *At Weddings and Wakes*. In *The Ninth Hour*, the experience is life-altering.

Sally's journey begins at New York City's Pennsylvania Station, entrance to the transit underworld, which, as Mary Gordon points out, "seems to be a branch of the Hieronymus Bosch Railroad Company."[12] In this subterranean realm, darkness contends with light: "The train was making its way through the tunnel that would lead them out of the city, passing through flashing columns of darkness and light. Of course, she had been riding subways all her life. She was as accustomed to being underground as any New Yorker. But that wing-stroke of terror . . . reverberated. . . . She had never before considered the fearful, foolish miracle of moving through this hollowed-out place" (*NH* 137–38). The subway causes Sally to think of the grave in which her father has lain for her whole life. "Never before" has she "equated its rushing darkness, its odor of soot and soil and steel, with the realm of the dead, the underside of bright cemeteries" (*NH* 138). Moving through her life, she merely visited lower regions "as she went blithely down the subway steps or down into the convent basement" (*NH* 138); at the same time, her father lay rotting in his grave. This is ironically a fitting fate for him; his job took him underground (he was a "motorman for the BRT" [*NH* 33], a New York City subway line), now he is underground through all time. As a Catholic, Sally has been taught to believe in the resurrection of the body, but she cannot turn her mind from the inexorable physical processes operating upon her father's body. Her inability to recover from this dreadful realization might account for her midlife depression.

Like the pit Odysseus digs, the underground world of Sally's train contains a variety of people, two of whom will tell their stories verbally and two nonverbally. The first and most significant of these is the "plump lady with two bulky shopping bags" (*NH* 136). Sally's panicked reaction to this "monster" suggests that this encounter will not go well.[13] The violation of physical boundaries inevitable when a fat lady with two large bags tries to fit into a small seat is as nothing compared to the woman's transgression of social boundaries. Upon learning that Sally was traveling with the intention of entering the convent, the plump lady somehow finds it appropriate to hold forth, complete with hand gestures, on the disappointing size of her husband's penis, for which flaw she is leaving him. She further elaborates upon her intention not to bleach her pubic hair blond, to match the new hair color she plans to get upon her arrival in California. After a bathroom joke and a harsh warning to Sally not to touch her possessions, she departs to the restroom. In a silent acknowledgment of the strangeness of the situation, "the man across the aisle lowered his newspaper and looked at Sally with a kind of amused sympathy" (*NH* 144).

Sally's fellow passengers also include a dirty-faced child, his head partially shaven and scabby, his teeth crooked, his body exhibiting marks of neglect and abuse, presumably by his parents. His story need not be spoken aloud as it is manifest in his appearance. The child is damaged, the child's mother is herself physically distorted, moving along the train aisle in a "stooped, hunchbacked way" (*NH* 146). Again "the man across the aisle" wordlessly acknowledges the situation. To escape these grotesques, Sally moves along the train aisle to the restroom, itself a stinking, foul pit. On this little journey within the longer journey, she meets yet another grotesque, "a man, smelling of alcohol, [who] passed by her too closely and rubbed his chest against hers, breathing into her face" (*NH* 146). The dirty child, the child's mother, and the reeking man are all comparable to the minor spirits Odysseus meets, the plump lady to the more fully developed underworld characters.

Moving further along, Sally arrives at the dining car, where she meets another character comparable to the plump lady, "a girl her own age" (*NH* 146), who also tells her story and whose story also transgresses normal social boundaries. The girl's sexual hunger for her husband has led her to steal her mother's silver tea set to pay her fare to Chicago, where the husband says he has found a job. That money is not enough, and the girl begs money from Sally as well. Sally is faced with a moral choice: "She knew that she should have the grace to give the girl all she had, as Christ would have done," but "she didn't want to . . . give up what her mother had so carefully saved. Didn't want—even more fiercely—to be mocked by another dirty stranger" (*NH* 151). Jesus tells his followers to sell all they have and give to the poor, but who counts as a worthy object of charity, as opposed to a "dirty stranger"? Is this girl a faker? Her appearance is not repulsive, but her behavior is. Sally makes a moral compromise, giving the girl only part of her money, silently castigating herself for lying. With that, the "man on the aisle" again reappears, "to steady her, and briefly, although she didn't need to, she gripped his hand. Warm and broad and very strong" (*NH* 154). Earlier in the trip Sally had lied to the conductor that her father was on the train. What Sally needs is the steadiness and strength of a father; failing that, the man on the aisle serves as a temporary substitute.

The alternation between light and darkness and the various noxious smells of the train combine with the grotesque characters to create a nightmarish atmosphere. The plump lady's refusing to move herself, or move her large bags, enrages Sally, and Sally, uncharacteristically, responds with violence and punches her. The plump lady proclaims her a devil, and Sally accepts this definition of herself. The whole experience on the train has become a descent into hell, and, like Odysseus, Sally is overwhelmed. "Fire and brimstone. It seemed the right smell for this hellish train, this terrible journey that could not have taken her farther from the convent's clean laundry and the pretty joy she had felt just this afternoon about the consecrated life she was called to" (*NH* 158). "It was three in the morning" (*NH* 158), the diametrical opposite of the ninth hour so sacred to God. The laundry analogy that Sally had come to believe in the convent basement has convinced her, in her youthful naïveté, that the gift of her own life would be a remedy applied "like a clean cloth to a seeping wound" (*NH* 153). The train ride has caused her to question and ultimately reject this belief. She realizes she has lost her faith in the possibility of purity and health in a filthy and diseased world.

These grotesques from the subterranean world join other exemplars of the filth and ugliness of human evil. Early in the novel, Annie witnesses a man beating a child; Sister Lucy discovers that an otherwise attractive young man, "Handsome Charlie" (*NH* 121), is abusing his sisters. These are not typical McDermott characters, most of whom in earlier novels are flawed but not evil. The child beater and the sister abuser are clearly evil, but the most significant, and most ambiguous, moral dilemma in the novel concerns Mrs. Costello. Is she as distorted morally as she is damaged physically?

Mrs. Costello's physical condition is described in revolting detail. Sally, shadowing the nuns in her early efforts to test her vocation, sees "Sister Lucy with the naked woman struggling in her arms. The contrast of the nun's broad black back, solid and shapeless in her veil, and the woman's thin, bare, flailing white extremities was grotesque, startling" (*NH* 99). Everything about Mrs. Costello is ugly: her "dry, mean, and thin" lips; her skeletal face; "barely a wisp of a body . . . no chest and narrow hips and only one good leg" (*NH* 224–25). Everything about Mrs. Costello is disgusting, not just because of appearance or because of her need for assistance with private bodily functions but because she is a person of weak character, self-absorbed, unappreciative of the help of others, unwilling to make any effort to help herself or to make herself useful in any way. If it is the duty of the able-bodied to help the sick, the sick also have a reciprocal duty to behave as well as they can. But Mrs. Costello gives her caretakers no gratification. She complains, within Sally's hearing, about the way Sally has done her hair. With the nuns, she is complaining, whining, demanding, bossy, negative, ungrateful, "childish, childishly exasperated" (*NH* 97); her crying, her "peevishness" (*NH* 106), her self-pity try the patience even of Sister Lucy.

Sister Lucy's judgment of Mrs. Costello is harsh. To her, suffering is no excuse for bad behavior. Because Mrs. Costello is still getting her period, Sister Lucy scorns her for a malingerer who should long ago have gotten over her injury and amputation and resumed a normal sex life and perhaps even had a baby. Since Mrs. Costello is obnoxious enough to try the patience of a nun, useless in the world and destructive of the happiness of others, does her life hold any redeeming value? The answer to that question depends on the characters' belief in an afterlife of either reward or punishment.

The "Glorious Impossible": Theories of the Hereafter

In her essay "Redeemed from Death? The Faith of a Catholic Novelist" (2013), Alice McDermott reflects on a consistent theme in her fiction, the immortality of the soul:

> From time to time in my fiction I have attempted to capture some sense of what it means to believe what we Catholics claim to believe. In *That Night,* it was a teenage girl who tells her troubled boyfriend that because she loves him he will not die. In *Charming Billy,* it's the alcoholic who believes that to become reconciled to the death of the young woman he loved is to diminish the injustice of it, and so to make Christ's sacrifice on the Cross unnecessary. In *After This,* a family's loyalty to an unlovable woman offers them an unexpected grace, a respite from their own inconsolable sorrow—love redeems them.[14]

McDermott offers reflections on immortality in these and other novels. In *A Bigamist's Daughter,* Tupper Daniels expresses his belief that true immortality resides in literature, a viewpoint that the otherwise not particularly religious narrator finds pitiable. In *That Night,* Sheryl believes that the intensity of human love is a proof of the immortality of the soul. In the same novel, the narrator is inspired by Sheryl's story to hope that her aborted fetus will be restored to her. In *After This,* John Keane develops his own theology of the afterlife: "all of us are immortal or no one is" (*AT* 55). In *Someone,* death and loss permeate the novel's atmosphere, but Marie ponders "all the faith and all the fancy, all the fear, the speculation, all the wild imaginings that go into the study of heaven and hell" (*S* 10). In *The Ninth Hour,* both Sally and Sister Jeanne believe in an afterlife and make "choices . . . in which the stakes are the highest" not just in this life but in the next.[15]

Sister Jeanne too has a theory of the afterlife, and hers is based on the concept of fairness: "Fairness demanded that grief should find succor, that wounds should heal, insult and confusion find recompense and certainty, that every living person God had made should not, willy-nilly, be forever unmade" (*NH* 53). This "quest for cosmic balance" seems in itself evidence of an afterlife in which all wrongs will be righted.[16] But Sister Jeanne does not believe that her fairness theory applies to suicides like Jim: "His death was a whim of his own. His own choice. Who, in all fairness, could demand its restitution?" (*NH* 54). Everyone else will find the moral scales balanced because fairness demands it. And that is true even for those who, like Sally, are tempted to commit a murder: "'You did no harm, dear. Whatever you'd thought to do.' She said, 'God is fair. He knows the truth'" (*NH* 232). Jeanne disregards traditional Catholic teaching on intentionality, according to which the plan is itself seriously sinful even if it is never carried out.

As the novel ends, Sister Jeanne is trapped in another piece of her own heterodoxy: that divine fairness demands that for Sally's sake Sister Jeanne herself be punished for all eternity. Jeanne imagines herself as having made a bargain with the Almighty: condemn me to hell that my beloved Sally may be saved. She does not ask for forgiveness, believing that she alone of all humankind has committed the unpardonable sin. But the Church "teaches explicitly that there is *no sin,* no matter how serious, that cannot be forgiven."[17] Might God be fairer than Jeanne herself can imagine? Would God not see Sister Jeanne's love for Sally as in itself redemptive? *The Ninth Hour* invites readers to consider such ultimate issues; nothing less will do.

Seven years before *The Ninth Hour* was published, Meoghan B. Cronin set forth the background against which "convent fiction" can be read: "the role of the nun in community and the conflicting though confluent development of girlhood and sisterhood."[18] Nuns, living in a female microcosm, "define themselves apart from marriage and men,"[19] their whole lives a testimony to a religious form of feminism. The coming of age of the young girls like Sally, entrusted to the nuns' care, involves a conflict between becoming a woman like Liz Tierney, on the one hand, or like any of the nuns, on the other. In *At Weddings and Wakes,* the children's catechism contains two pictures: "one of a woman serving her family their dinner—'This is good' printed beneath—the other of a nun receiving Communion from a priest: 'This is better'" (58). Sally confronts the same choice, with all of the guilt implied in choosing that which is merely good over that which is better. While Sally eventually opts for the life of a wife and mother, her midlife depression may be the heritage not only of her father's suicide but of her upbringing as a convent child.

CHAPTER 10

The Short Fiction

Alice McDermott has published fifteen short stories, as yet uncollected, dating from 1979 on; for many writers, these alone would constitute a significant body of work. Since McDermott's claim to literary recognition rests on her novels, however, her short stories are examined here mainly as they relate to the longer fictions. The approach, like that used by the author herself, is not chronological but moves back and forth in time between different works to illustrate the way in which McDermott's body of work forms a coherent whole.

Time and Tides on "The Island"

Island settings in literature are often self-contained microcosms that represent the larger world. The geography of Long Island suits this fictional purpose, near to—but apart from—the world's largest city. Its climate provides a convenient metaphor for the passage of time and the transitory nature of human happiness. The all-too-brief summer season, with its trips to the Island's many attractive beaches, is the high point of the year, but implicit even in those moments is the imminent arrival of autumn and, finally, a cold, bleak winter. The summer beach scene in McDermott's fiction often suggests a local version of the Garden of Eden from which a fall from grace is inevitable. The beach in summer often references young love and hope, while the beach in autumn conjures up feelings of nostalgia and regret.

In "Small Losses" (1979), a teenage girl, who in some ways resembles McDermott's fifteen-year-old protagonist Theresa in *Child of My Heart,* sits on her beach blanket and fantasizes about the perfect summer romance, with a boy who is the very personification of summer, "perfect—bronzed by the sun, fun-loving, caring" (150). Even a girl as young as she is realizes that "there would be moments of sadness too" (150); nevertheless, she anticipates the arrival of her teenage Prince Charming. Two boys happen by, flatter the protagonist, and seem to hint at future meetings but instead steal her soda and animal crackers and disappear. The material loss to the young girl is "small," but she also loses the bright hope that the season promises.

McDermott's sensitivity to the feelings of teenagers appears later, in the story "I Am Awake" (2009), in the novel *That Night* (1987) and the film made from it (1992), and in the essay "Teen-Age Films: Love, Death and the Prom" (1987). The contrast between the bright hope of the summer romance and the inevitable betrayal is an important element in the story of Billy and Eva in *Charming Billy,* made even more poignant by the fact that Billy is no starry-eyed teenager but a grown man, a veteran back from the war. Beach settings play an important role also in *At Weddings and Wakes* as the North Fork / South Fork vacation venues of the Dailey family; in *Child of My Heart,* much of which involves beach trips with children in tow; and in *After This,* in which an early autumn trip to the beach prompts a meditation on the passage of time.

Beach communities often feature a division between the year-round residents and the "summer people," who represent the transience of all things. "Summer Folk" (1981) focuses on sixty-eight-year-old Will, a year-rounder in a beach town who experiences the typical losses consequent not just on the change of seasons but on the passage of time: "his daughter was grown . . . his wife dead nearly two years . . . he was retired from Grumman [an aerospace corporation then headquartered in Bethpage] and living alone" (69). It being late spring, "the last few cool days and slow, silent weekends before the summer crowd arrived" (72), his niece arrives with two friends in search of a cottage to rent. The evening he spends with them enables him to acknowledge that, although "summer folk" come with the season, they always leave, and, in the autumn of the year and of his life, he will be alone again.

While Will and his guests jokingly toast each other's tribes, the year-rounders and the summer people, the two groups are often at odds. The social class differences in these communities are clearly indicated by their respective houses. A house like Will's, a modest cottage on the edges of a wealthier community, reappears in *Charming Billy* as Holtzman's house, to which Billy and Dennis return after the war. This house is near the larger, more elaborate summer homes such as the one owned by the wealthy family for which Eva works as a nanny. Holtzman's house assumes a symbolic significance for Billy, as the essence of all life's joys, and he vows not to return to this cottage out of grief for Eva. Dennis and Maeve, who do not allow grief and loss to define them, make it their permanent home in the autumn of their lives. In *Child of My Heart,* Theresa's family's small year-round house is near the lavish home of the artist whose wife employs Theresa as a babysitter. The social differences in the community are manifest in the relative size of the houses. The year-rounders provide temporary domestic services to the transients, thus reinforcing class boundaries.

The details of beach life with children constitute much of the plot of *Child of My Heart,* Small variations in the weather dictate what can and cannot be done on any given day, and the complicated mechanics of beach-going are described in detail. It is a judgment on their parenting that, in a community in which the beach is the central attraction and proximity to it a barometer of real estate value, the artist and his wife outsource their child's beach visits to the babysitter and never take the child themselves. In *After This,* the parents are middle class and thus do take their own children to the beach, even though it is a longer trip, and even in the autumn.

"Summer Folk" also introduces a recurrent topic of conversation for McDermott's characters as for their real-life counterparts on Long Island: traffic and the ingenious stratagems devised to evade it. The automotive comings and goings in the novels are often specified as to route and can be traced on a map of Long Island, as, for example, Elizabeth and Tupper's trip to the Hamptons in *A Bigamist's Daughter* and Tom Commeford's trip to retrieve Gabe from "Suffolk—the mental hospital out east" (*S* 199), named for the Island's easternmost county.

Telling Stories, Telling Lies

McDermott's novels contain many oral storytelling episodes—smaller, self-contained fictions within the larger fictions, told by particular characters to a particular listening audience. Because the nature of the storytelling situation depends on many factors—remembering, forgetting, omitting, revising, adjusting content to the listening audience, narrating different versions of the same story—the distinction between artistic license and outright deception is often blurred. The indistinct border between storytelling and falsehood is often a pivotal point in the plots of McDermott's novels, as is deliberate withholding of a story's important elements.

This recurrent motif is introduced in "The Simple Truth" (1978). In it, a woman conducts a love relationship with a young lawyer based on a false version of her own life. When, via a random phone call, he discovers that she has deceived him, he asks the obvious question: "What's the story?," which for him is synonymous with "Why did you lie?" (73). He is clearly demanding an explanation of her motives for creating a fictionalized character as a stand-in for her real self, and, what is worse, casting him without his knowledge in the role of that character's love interest. In this story the term "fiction" is identical in meaning to the term "lie" because the motive of the young woman is not to create art but to deceive. No "simple" explanation can repair the relationship.

In the novels, storytelling can involve deliberate lying. In *A Bigamist's Daughter,* Tupper Daniels, a writer, believes that he needs a story taken from life to provide an ending to his novel. To that end, he cultivates a relationship with a vanity press editor whose own father was a bigamist; that is, a man whose whole life was a lie similar to that of Daniels's fictional character. The relationship between Tupper and his editor may itself be a lie, a pretense to get access to the editor's father's story. In *Charming Billy,* Dennis's lie—that Eva has died in Ireland—is told from considerate motives but, in an outcome that Dennis could not foresee, causes Billy's own life for the next thirty years to be based on that fiction. In *The Ninth Hour,* Sister St. Saviour creates a counter-narrative of Jim's death to gain him burial in a Catholic cemetery but for the best of reasons: to protect his grief-stricken pregnant widow from the further pain of the heartless application of Church rules.

Storytelling is a way of transmitting family heritage and local lore. The story told in "Lost for the Holidays" (2005) is a childhood memory narrated by an old woman to her younger relatives. As a child, the narrator was taken on an outer-boroughs ritual, a holiday trip from Brooklyn to Manhattan. She visits St. Patrick's Cathedral, then Gimbels, and in the department store is separated from her mother and siblings. The child is traumatized: "what could compare with the terror of being a child lost on Christmas Eve?" (A17). The childhood fear is so vivid that she still feels "lost . . . waiting for them to find me" (A17), even in great old age. The tale-teller wants to give her tale "a Dickensian spin" (A17), reinventing her child self as one of the novelist's pathetic waifs in order to evoke maximum sympathy. But her younger family members have been desensitized by her too-frequent repetition of the story. Where she hopes for sympathy, they respond with indifference. They trivialize her childhood grief, attributing to the story no significance other than as a symptom of aging.

Unlike the reaction of the family members in "Lost for the Holidays," the children in two of McDermott's novels take the storyteller and the story seriously: in *At Weddings and Wakes,* the emigration story and death of Momma Towne's sister Annie is central to the family's history; and in *The Ninth Hour,* the story of Red Whelan shapes a family's understanding of itself. *Someone* also includes tales told by women in Fagin's and his mother's apartment over the funeral home, in which legends and lore of the community are preserved. No collection of tales would be complete without its ghost story, and that is provided in *At Weddings and Wakes* with the narrative of the mysterious figure in the window.

Love, Marriage, and Divorce

In her short fiction as well as her novels, McDermott has considered the dynamics of heterosexual love relationships. In "Romantic Reruns" (1979), the following question is posed: are intense feelings at the beginning of a love affair the best predictor of its success? Or is a sense of comfortable inevitability more important? Watching a rerun of an old film, Martha finds herself overwhelmed with emotion and judges her own relationships, with her current lover John and her former lover Mark, and even the "sexual chain letter" (66) that is her past, as inferior to the ones depicted in theater and film. She eventually marries Mark, but she still finds herself in the grip of romantic fantasies. Has she allowed herself to settle? She finds herself "wondering if this wasn't just the way it happened, the way a real love, a lifelong passion revealed itself: unexpectedly and with little emotion" (72). What is "real love?" Is it based on "grand passion," or is it merely "just a pleasant way to live" (62)?

These questions are relevant to discussing the married couples in McDermott's novels. In *That Night,* a teen romance is so intense as to involve a whole neighborhood but ends in suburban banality. Lucy and Bob Dailey's marriage in *At Weddings and Wakes* is neither passionate nor pleasant but suffers from a nameless malaise. Billy Lynch's ideal vision of Eva in *Charming Billy* can be contrasted to his apparently passionless but long-lasting marriage to Maeve and, later, Maeve's to Dennis. The two long-married couples in *After This* and *Someone* might also be evaluated along the "grand passion" versus "pleasant way to live" spectrum.

This passion-versus-practicality issue is considered also in "Not a Love Story" (1982), in which the protagonist has left her boyfriend, whom she found "merely . . . comfortable" (90); she has a new job in a new city; but, like the protagonist in "Romantic Reruns," she senses an emptiness. She is at a decision point in her life, in "limbo," at an age when her "child-bearing years [have] become a serious consideration" (190). Imagining herself as a character in a short story, she thinks of her life to that point as an extended exposition in which characters are introduced but nothing yet happens; a man must "enter to begin the plot," to trigger the rising action of a love story. The protagonist has left her "comfortable" boyfriend who "would have married her a year ago and given her a home" (90), but are comfort and shelter sufficient? Like the protagonist of "Romantic Reruns," she builds her self-concept on fictional models—in her case, Ernest Hemingway's women, always secondary characters, valuable only in their relationship to the macho hero. Will she have to choose between various minor characters in the drama of life, female stereotypes: "the efficient, celibate career woman . . . the woman who prides herself on knowing nothing but a different man each night . . . the lonely-eyed women in the chess class . . . the hollow-eyed women in the suburbs" (192)? Unconsciously modeling her life on that of a fairy-tale heroine, she longs for a man to transform her into the star of her own story.

Three of the female stereotypes mentioned in this story are not characteristic of McDermott's fiction thus far. She has no Hemingway heroines, fairy-tale princesses, or sexual free spirits. The fourth, the celibate, childless woman, is represented by Pauline in *After This,* and in some ways she is seen as perpetually incomplete, a secondary character ancillary to Mary Keane, wife and mother, significant only in her relationship to Mary's daughter, Clare.

McDermott has not yet explored in her fiction the type of conflicts between a woman's career and marriage/parenthood as experienced in reality by highly educated and accomplished women like the novelist herself. Her female protagonists to date have been women who are minimally educated, holding unchallenging jobs that they are contented to abandon for marriage and motherhood. This is consistent with her depiction of men. The world of high-powered careerists, female or male, is not the world of her fiction. Her men come from the same social background as the women; they work diligently at routine jobs, and several are good, if unexciting, husbands: Dennis Lynch in *Charming Billy,* John Keane in *After This,* and Tom Commeford in *Someone.* Even Mr. Costello, the adulterous milkman in *The Ninth Hour,* is a loyal caretaker of his disabled wife. The men who are even mildly exciting are also deeply flawed: the damaged Walter Harnett in *Someone,* the suicide Jim in *The Ninth Hour.*

Few of McDermott's characters experience marital discord severe enough to trigger divorce, the exceptions being Lucy and Bob Dailey in *At Weddings and Wake* and the Kaufmans in *Child of My Heart*. Their lives postdivorce do not form part of the narrative. In the short story "Deliveries" (1980), McDermott focuses on the difficulties an abandoned mother experiences in trying to support her young children by delivering newspapers before dawn. The title of the story plays on the obstetrical meaning of the term "deliveries." Having given birth to two children, mothers must cope; but fathers can just vanish, like the bigamist in McDermott's first novel. The logistics of safely transporting two sleeping children in the back of her station wagon is just one example of the many realistic domestic details that feature in McDermott's work. Another is the description of the household chaos wrought by young children: "the living room is filled with building blocks and crayons and scraps of paper. One crayon, bright orange, has been stepped on, crushed into the beige rug. There is baby food in her hair; she smells like squash" (148). The protagonist's husband left her because the exciting life they had planned together—the "lean and childless middle age, a life of art and good food and casual European travel" (148)—had devolved into the repetitive routines of parenthood. The minutiae of child care reappears in great quantity in *Child of My Heart,* limning the dullness of a day spent with small children. The economic differences between the parents of a toddler in *Child of My Heart* and in "Deliveries" mean that the former will hire a babysitter, housekeeper, and cook to endure the tedium while they pursue their own interests.

In "Deliveries," the young couple, in happier days, buys a suburban house, and "joke[s] that they would have to surround it with a white picket fence and twining rosebushes" (146). Gentle satire of the suburban lifestyle is part and parcel of McDermott's role as a local colorist. She also recognizes the malaise that is the downside of living in these bedroom communities. Such discontent permeates the atmosphere of "She Knew What She Wanted" (1986). Its setting is a town that is "not exclusive, but it does bask in the reflected glory of the small, famously posh town to our east" (44). So this is a town like the one in which the McDermott family vacationed, as described in her essay "Old Haunts" (2013); like the one wherein Billy meets Eva in *Charming Billy;* like the one in which Theresa's family lives in *Child of My* Heart; all of them very like Hampton Bays, a more affordable neighbor to the "famously posh" Southampton. In this typical Long Island town, an apparently successful marriage is threatened by a neighbor's desire to replace her current husband with that of the narrator. The husband, Brian, is in full midlife crisis mode. Leaving his wife and his two children for another (newer, wealthier, but essentially similar) woman symbolizes, for him, a new set of possibilities. Most of the married men in McDermott's novels (except Mr. Costello, in *The Ninth Hour*) are faithful husbands. They may note the passage of time, as does John Keane in the beach scene of *After This,* but do not see the dissolution of their marriages as a remedy for midlife melancholia.

"Home" (2016) returns to McDermott's novelistic home turf of Queens, to the "old neighborhood" motif recurrent in her fiction, and to the geographic specificity of a local colorist. The protagonist is a divorced man named Jim. His mother lives in a senior residence in Little Neck (only a five-minute drive along Northern Boulevard from Billy and Maeve's house in Bayside). Lee, Jim's mother's hairdresser's divorced daughter, lives with her own parents in Queens, while the protagonist lives in Hauppauge, in Suffolk County. Queens person that she is, Lee regards Hauppauge as "way out in the country" (it is actually thirty miles from Little Neck, which is on the Queens side of the Queens/ Nassau border). As a young girl, she refused to apply to be an NBC page on the grounds of inaccessibility: "I'm not going all the way in to Rockefeller Center" (in Manhattan, requiring a commute on the Long Island Railroad, then a subway). These geographical details characterize Lee as limited in ways other than spatial. She relocated out west with her ex-husband, but "never felt at home." Despite her miserable mother, Lee regards her parents' house as "home," a place of refuge from her equally miserable marriage. Jim too, although once a Queens native, cannot now imagine feeling "at home" anyplace else but Hauppauge. As the title suggests, "home" is a state of mind, as both Lee and Jim compensate for their failed marriages by reaffirming their connection with a precise geographical location.

This story contains characters and situations that are recapitulated in McDermott's novels. Lee's verbally abusive mother, though she believes herself to be a martyr to her daughter, is a forerunner of the moral grotesques, Mrs. Costello and the fat lady on the train, in *The Ninth Hour.* The mindset that one of the urban boroughs is the center of the universe is found in Marie's reluctance to leave Brooklyn, even just for the workday, in *Someone.* Lee's difficult childbirth is similar to those of Mary Keane in *After This* and of Marie Commeford and Gerty Hanson's mother in *Someone.*

In "Robert of the Desert" (1989), the return of the protagonist's brother Robert to New York from an extended work assignment in Saudi Arabia is comparable to the soon-to-be-divorced Lois's own return to the land of the unattached. His return reminds her of how civility and order are missing both from New York City and from her own life. She has abandoned her marriage because she was tired of it and finds no satisfaction in either her job or her new lover. Both she and her brother are returning to a place, geographically and psychologically, that they thought they had abandoned long before and must find their way amid the sort of ethical confusion of which Manhattan traffic is a suitable metaphor. Here, as in "Home" and in *At Weddings and Wakes,* emotional dislocation is explored in geographical terms. Memory, too, one of McDermott's continuous concerns, operates in this story in that the encounter with her brother causes her to see the roots of her malaise in childhood memories, particularly of her parents' relationship with her and with each other.

Rites of Passage

Deaths, funerals, and other rituals of mourning feature prominently throughout McDermott's fiction: the protagonist's mother's funeral in *A Bigamist's Daughter,* contrasting with the lack of due ceremony surrounding the death of her father; Sheryl's father's death in *That Night;* the death of Annie and Jack Towne and Momma Towne's recurrent summonses to funerals of remote acquaintances, as well as that of the newlywed May, in *At Weddings and Wakes;* Billy's funeral, the restaurant luncheon, the gathering at Maeve's house thereafter, and the graveside ceremony at the burial of Uncle Daniel, all in *Charming Billy;* Billy's misguided care of Eva's supposed grave in the same novel; the many dead children, especially Daisy, in *Child of My Heart;* the death in childbirth of Gerty Hanson's mother and the funeral of Jacob in *After This;* Marie's work as "consoling angel" in Fagin's funeral home, her father's death, the wakes for Pegeen Chehab and for Bill Corrigan, the tales of the dead told in Mrs. Fagin's apartment in *Someone;* the death of Mrs. Costello, the truncated ritual for the suicide of Jim, the elder Patrick Tierney's funeral in *The Ninth Hour.*

McDermott examines the rituals of mourning in her short fiction as well. In "I Am Awake" (2009), teenagers, new to sorrow, devise their own ritual for a dead classmate. At Jake Barry's funeral, Irish American traditions of mourning, including a song in Irish, "human and beautiful and full of sorrow" (20), produce reactions similar to that produced by "Billy Sheehy's dad, all unrehearsed" (*CB* 138), singing "Danny Boy" at Uncle Daniel's funeral in *Charming Billy.* The song seems to console the adults, as do the predictable eulogies. But these traditional expressions of grief do not satisfy the adolescents' need for a communal ritual of their own involving clandestine, and prohibited, midnight visits to the boy's gravesite. Earlier in her career, in *That Night,* McDermott paid respectful attention to the emotions of teenagers in love, relationships that are often trivialized, and this story validates their way of grieving, bizarre as it may seem to the adult world. The customary duration of funerary rituals is too brief to accommodate their mourning, so, even a year later and despite all the distracting events of senior year, Jake's friends are still visiting his grave in the nighttime, still not ready to "give him up yet."

In "Desired Things" (2016), a long-married couple faces the approach of death in a commonplace setting. The story narrates the onset of dementia in an elderly husband. Driving along the New Jersey Turnpike from a wedding on Long Island to their home in Virginia, the wife notices "the altered Manhattan skyline" (24) after the 2001 attacks on the World Trade Center. At the rest stop, she observes a family sharing a meal with their adult child who has Down syndrome, which the wife thinks must be another kind of loss, a "disappointment," a daily source of "regret" for "what might have been for their damaged child" (26). Both images—the vanished twin towers and the Down syndrome man—are a reminder of the precarious nature of good fortune. Having just come from a wedding at which the best man gave a minimalist toast—"You're married now. Good luck with that" (25)—the wife thinks about the important role luck plays in a marriage. She and her husband have been among the fortunate in life, but just as the young man's Down syndrome is caused by, in the husband's words, "life. Biology. The luck of the draw" (26) in the nature of things, the luck of this aging couple cannot last forever. As the husband emerges from the restroom, he is disoriented, his dementia having surfaced for the first time; this day is "the beginning of their long fall" (26). A wedding has been the prelude to a wake.

"You Will Be Missed" (2014), another funeral story, has elements in common with scenes in several of McDermott's novels. In the story, sixteen-year-old Brian is awakened on a Saturday morning for the funeral of a man he never met. This leads to Brian's observation of the paradoxical behavior of a brother and sister, his father and aunt, who, though both living on the same long, narrow Long Island for thirty-seven years, have not seen each other due to a vaguely described conflict. Despite this long separation, Michael, Brian's father, decides to take his youngest son to the funeral of his sister's husband, Hugh. The son is baffled: "What kind of people don't see their only sibling for years, then show up at her husband's funeral? What kind of Irish joke are you?" (15). A young boy learns the customs of the tribe by observing the minutiae of Catholic funerary ritual: the altar, the holy water, the kneeling bench, the candles. But he also has a spiritual experience, a reminder of personal mortality. The deceased's name is Hugh, which means that the priest's elegy serves as a *memento mori* not only for him but for all members of the congregation: "Hugh will be missed" (16).

In *The Ninth Hour,* Michael Tierney takes his son Patrick to the funeral of his own father, also named Patrick, from whom he, like the brother and sister in "You Will Be Missed," has been estranged for most of his adult life, and the young man must grow in understanding of his family through that experience. The story in "You Will Be Missed" of "the legendary Uncle Jim" who with his wife raised Michael and his sister, Bronagh, after the deaths of their parents, is featured in the family's narrative of itself, like the tales of the past in *At Weddings and Wakes* and of Red Whelan in *The Ninth Hour.* As in the novel as well, unanswered questions remain about the mysterious ways of this family: What caused the estrangement of brother and sister? Why does Brian's mother not attend? Are Brian's parents both alcoholics, as rumor has it? As in *At Weddings and Wakes,* because a funeral serves as a family reunion, perceived resemblances compensate at least partially for long-damaged ties and reaffirm the connections between members of the tribe.

Spirituality of Everyday Life

In all her novels, Alice McDermott explores the spirituality of the commonplace. This central theme is not explored in comparable depth in her short fiction, with two exceptions. In "Enough" (2000), McDermott's most-anthologized story to date, a child's love for the once-a-month treat of ice cream for Sunday dessert presages her lust for all life's sensual pleasures. When sensual pleasure turns sexual and more than ice cream is involved, she must come to terms with the guilt and shame culture of Irish American Catholicism. The story, with its delight in a life well lived, whether in bed with her husband or raiding the refrigerator for frozen treats, contains an implied critique of the Church's discomfort with physical pleasure.

What the family euphemistically refers to as the nameless protagonist's "trouble with the couch," upon which she enjoys an encounter with a neighbor boy, results in "a good soaking in recriminations" (82) administered by both her mother and the priest in confession. Both are wrong, however. Her lust for life serves her well in adult life, as she welcomes seven children and enjoys a robust sex life with her husband until death parts them. Thereafter, well into her eighties, she reverts to her earlier source of pleasure, ice cream, but to such an extent that the new puritans, her health-conscious children and grandchildren, try to limit her intake. Earthly pleasures, whether "forbidden youthful passion and domestic married love," or ice cream, all are seen in the story not as occasions of sin but rather as intimations of immortality. In life, though there is "plenty to satisfy," there is "never enough" (85), and this insufficiency is itself a hint at the possibility of an afterlife.

"Gloria" (2014) is set, untypically for McDermott, not on Long Island but in Washington, DC, close to McDermott's home as of this writing in Bethesda, Maryland. An affluent family gathers at Thanksgiving, a secular holiday, and the family itself is secular, having long ago abandoned religious practice. Via a slip of the tongue during the toast, the family's patriarch, Richard, describes the family not as "lucky," as he had intended, but "blessed." The mistake triggers an internal conflict within Richard: "he felt, as soon as he uttered the word, a shaft of cold air, as if a small pane of glass in the mullioned window at the end of the elegant room had been punched out by an invisible hand" (A17). The transcendent inserts itself into, asserts itself within, ordinary life—like it or not. And Richard is not at all comfortable with this experience.

Richard's unintended words also have the dual effect of triggering a conflict with his son's fiancée, Gloria. Given her own family's sad history, Gloria cannot believe in the concept of blessing as a sign of God's favor—indeed, she resents the idea that "God somehow favors" some, but not her parents, who suffered terribly despite being "good people who worked hard" (A17). Gloria resents also the theological implications of a blessing, which requires the existence of a Someone, "whoever it is who does the blessing" (A17) but also withholds it, in a fashion that to humans seems painfully arbitrary. Richard's son, Gloria's fiancé, tries to salvage the social moment, but in doing so he inadvertently trivializes a theological problem as old as the Book of Job: the existence of evil in a world created and ruled by an omnipotent and loving God. Why do some suffer, seemingly undeservedly? Is earthly success and happiness a sign of God's favor? The father did not even intend to raise this issue: "it was a toast he had stood to offer, a Thanksgiving toast. No one had asked him for a prayer" (A17). Once he uses the language of prayer, he introduces a spiritual dilemma into a secular holiday. The story ends, like the Book of Job, without an answer, at least not one comprehensible to mere mortals.

NOTES

Chapter 1—Understanding Alice McDermott

1. McDermott, "In Praise of Great Teachers."
2. Osen, "Alice McDermott," 112.
3. Lewis, "Class Act."
4. Smith, "Alice McDermott."
5. Smith, "Alice McDermott."
6. Smith, "Writers Online."
7. Contino, "Conversation with Alice McDermott," 66.
8. Treisman, "This Week in Fiction."
9. McDermott, "Annual Sermon, Retold."
10. McDermott, "Night without End."
11. Smith, "Writers Online."
12. Osen, "Alice McDermott," 114.
13. McDermott, "Redeemed from Death?," 16.
14. Contino, "Conversation with Alice McDermott," 66.
15. Contino, "Conversation with Alice McDermott," 71.
16. McDermott, "Confessions of a Reluctant Catholic."
17. McDermott, "Confessions of a Reluctant Catholic."
18. Gray, "Family Album."

Chapter 2—*A Bigamist's Daughter* (1982)

1. Smith, "Alice McDermott."
2. Ellin, "The Gloves Are Definitely Gone."
3. Smith, "Alice McDermott."
4. Third Plenary Council of Baltimore, *A Catechism of Christian Doctrine.*
5. McCartin, "Unto Dust."
6. Tyler, "Novels by Three Emerging Writers."
7. Tyler, "Novels by Three Emerging Writers."
8. Osen, interview with McDermott, 118; italics in original.
9. McDermott, "Redeemed from Death?," 16.
10. Contino, "Conversation with Alice McDermott," 69.

Chapter 3—*That Night* (1987)

1. Smith, "Alice McDermott."
2. Smith, "Alice McDermott."
3. Jurca, "White Diaspora," 8–9.

4. Moynihan, "'None of Us Will Always Be Here,'" 45.
5. Smith, "Alice McDermott."
6. McDermott, foreword to *City Lights,* xiii.
7. Leavitt, "Fathers, Daughters, and Hoodlums."
8. Eder, review of *That Night,* 3.
9. Bolotin, *That Night.*

Chapter 4—*At Weddings and Wakes* (1991)

1. Coughlan, "Paper Ghosts," 124.
2. Smith, "Writers Online."
3. Osen, "Alice McDermott," 119.
4. Osen, "Alice McDermott," 118.
5. Farnsworth, "Alice McDermott."
6. Smith, "Writers Online."
7. Vejvoda, "'Too Much Knowledge of the Other World,'" 42; and Harvey, *Contemporary Irish Traditional Narrative,* 5.
8. Jacobson, "Alice McDermott's Narrators," 120.
9. Smith, "Writers Online."
10. Harvey, *Contemporary Irish Traditional Narrative,* 7.
11. Harney, *Contemporary Irish Traditional Narrative,* 14.
12. Harvey, *Contemporary Irish Traditional Narrative,* 8.
13. Shannon, *American Irish,* 25.
14. Nolan, *Ourselves Alone,* 73.
15. Miller, *Emigrants and Exiles,* 273; and Diner, *Erin's Daughters in America,* 36.
16. Diner, *Erin's Daughters in America,* 84–85.
17. Murphy, "Bridie, We Hardly Knew Ye," 144.
18. Miller, *Emigrants and Exiles,* 505.
19. Lysaght, *Pocket Book of the Banshee,* 7.
20. Lysaght, *Pocket Book of the Banshee,* 24.
21. Quoted in Lysaght, *Pocket Book of the Banshee,* 28, 31.
22. Quoted in Lysaght, *Pocket Book of the Banshee,* 24.
23. McGlynn, "Gush of Wind as an Omen of Death," 1309.
24. Lysaght, *Pocket Book of the Banshee,* 29.
25. Lysaght, *Pocket Book of the Banshee,* 86.
26. Lysaght, *Pocket Book of the Banshee,* 15.
27. Lysaght, *Pocket Book of the Banshee,* 30.
28. Lysaght, *Pocket Book of the Banshee,* 53.
29. Crabtree-Sinnett, "Piety, Innocence, and Irishness," 45–46.
30. Diner, *Erin's Daughters in America,* 39.
31. Quinn, *Looking for Jimmy,* 41.
32. Diner, *Erin's Daughters in America,* 43.
33. Carden, "Making Love, Making History," 10; Coughlan, "Paper Ghosts," 133; and Crabtree-Sinnett, "Condition of Permanent Mourning."
34. Steinfels, "Archeology of Yearning," 102.
35. Steinfels, "Archeology of Yearning," 102.
36. Diner, *Erin's Daughters in America,* 13.
37. Jurca, "White Diaspora," 8.
38. Jurca, "White Diaspora," 8.

39. Coughlan, "Paper Ghosts," 128.
40. Coughlan, "Paper Ghosts," 128.

Chapter 5—*Charming Billy* (1998)

1. On McDermott's place within the Catholic literary tradition, see Gioia, "Catholic Writer Today"; Wolfe, "Catholic Writer, Then and Now"; and O'Connell, "'Glorious Impossible.'"
2. McDermott, "Confessions of a Reluctant Catholic."
3. McDermott, "Lunatic in the Pew."
4. Steinfels, "Archeology of Yearning," 100.
5. McDermott, "Confessions of a Reluctant Catholic."
6. McDermott, "Confessions of a Reluctant Catholic."
7. Osen, "Alice McDermott," 117.
8. Coughlan, "Paper Ghosts," 138.
9. Coughlan, "Paper Ghosts," 138.
10. Steinfels, "Archeology of Yearning," 100.
11. Contino, "Conversation with Alice McDermott," 66; cf. Steinfels, "Archeology of Yearning," 94.
12. McDermott, "Lunatic in the Pew."
13. Treisman, "This Week in Fiction."
14. Contino, "Conversation with Alice McDermott," 67.
15. McDermott, "Lunatic in the Pew."
16. Hallissy, "Bringing Paddies Over," 143–145.
17. McDermott, "Lunatic in the Pew."
18. McCartin, "Unto Dust."
19. McCartin, "Unto Dust."
20. Carden, "Making Love, Making History," 14.
21. S. O'Connell, "That Much Credit," 265.
22. *Merriam-Webster Dictionary;* my italics.
23. McCartin, "Unto Dust."
24. Gioia, "Catholic Writer Today," 35.

Chapter 6—*Child of My Heart* (2002)

1. Jones, "All Sugar, No Spice," 80.
2. Deignan, "A World Away," 26.
3. Jacobson, "Alice McDermott's Narrators," 133.
4. Carden, "Kingdom by the Sea," 246.
5. Smith, "Writers Online."
6. Corso, "Allie, Phoebe, Robert Emmet, and Daisy Mae," 94.
7. Hagan, "American Wake," 198.
8. Carden, "Kingdom by the Sea," 247.
9. Jacobson, "Alice McDermott's Narrators," 122.
10. Corso, "Allie, Phoebe, Robert Emmet, and Daisy Mae," 105.
11. Corso, "Psychoanalysing Theresa," 27.
12. Hagan, "American Wake," 200.
13. Carden, "Kingdom by the Sea," 251.
14. Carden, "Kingdom by the Sea," 253.
15. Hagan, "American Wake," 194.

16. Carden, "Kingdom by the Sea," 256.
17. Hagan, "American Wake," 195.
18. Carden, "Kingdom by the Sea," 256.
19. Corso, "Allie, Phoebe, Robert Emmet, and Daisy Mae," 95–96.

Chapter 7—*After This* (2006)

1. López, "Reverberant Music," 238.
2. López, "Reverberant Music," 238–39.
3. Thurston, "Honouring the Ordinary," 538.
4. Thurston, "Honouring the Ordinary," 539, citing *AT* 186.
5. Anderson, "*After This* by Alice McDermott."
6. Myers, "Novelist Alice McDermott."

Chapter 8—*Someone* (2013)

1. Cohen, "The Drift of Years."
2. O'Connell, "'Glorious Impossible,'" 501, citing *S*8.
3. Contino, "Gleams of Life Everlasting," 507.
4. O'Connell, "'Glorious Impossible,'" 503.
5. October 28, 2017.

Chapter 9—*The Ninth Hour* (2017)

1. McAlpin, "Tonic for the Ills of the World."
2. Gordon, "In Alice McDermott's Novel."
3. Thurston, "Honouring the Ordinary," 538.
4. Crowe, "*Ninth Hour,*" 43.
5. Crowe, "*Ninth Hour,*" 43.
6. O'Reilly, "Nothing To Be Done?," 37.
7. Shank, "In the Old Neighborhoods of Brooklyn," 52.
8. Kane and Tuohey, "Suicide."
9. McDermott, "Confessions of a Reluctant Catholic."
10. See Begley, "Grace and Gumption," 67.
11. Homer, *Odyssey*, translated by Stanley Lombardo, 411.
12. Gordon, "In Alice McDermott's Novel."
13. Gordon, "In Alice McDermott's Novel."
14. McDermott, "Redeemed from Death?," 16.
15. Gordon, "In Alice McDermott's Novel."
16. Shank, "Sister Knows Best," 53.
17. Halle, "Can Every Sin Be Forgiven?," 49, citing *The Catechism of the Catholic Church*.
18. Cronin, "Maiden Mothers and Little Sisters," 263.
19. Cronin, "Maiden Mothers and Little Sisters," 264.

BIBLIOGRAPHY

Works by Alice McDermott

NOVELS

After This. New York: Farrar, 2006. Abbreviated *AT* in text.
At Weddings and Wakes. New York: Picador, 1992. Abbreviated *AWAW* in text.
A Bigamist's Daughter. New York: Dell / Random House, 1982. Abbreviated *BD* in text.
Charming Billy. New York: Picador, 1998. Abbreviated *CB* in text.
Child of My Heart. New York: Picador, 2002. Abbreviated *CH* in text.
The Ninth Hour. New York: Farrar, 2017. Abbreviated *NH* in text.
Someone. New York: Farrar, 2013. Abbreviated *S* in text.
That Night. New York: Dell / Random House, 1987. Abbreviated *TN* in text.

SHORT FICTION

"Deliveries." *Redbook,* July 1980, 29, 145–46, 148.
"Desired Things." *Commonweal,* November 11, 2016, 24–26.
"Enough," *New Yorker,* April 10, 2000, 82–85.
———. In *The Long Meanwhile: Stories of Arrival and Departure,* edited by Shelley Jackson and Lydia Davis, 1–9. Lindenhurst, IL: Hourglass Books, 2007.
———. In *More Stories We Tell: The Best Contemporary Short Stories by North American Women*, edited by Wendy Martin, 231–38. New York: Pantheon Books, 2004.
———. In *Secret Ingredients: The New Yorker Book of Food and Drink,* edited by David Remnick, 545–51. New York: Modern Library, 2008.
———. In *Selected Shorts: Food Fictions.* New York: Symphony Space, 2007.
"Gloria." *Washington Post,* November 14, 2014, A17.
"Home." *Harper's Magazine,* September 2016, 69–74.
"I Am Awake." *Commonweal,* July 17, 2009, 16–21.
"Lost for the Holidays." *New York Times,* December 24, 2005, A17.
"Not a Love Story." *Mademoiselle,* February 1982, 90, 190, 192.
"Robert of the Desert." *Savvy Woman,* July 1989, 62–68.
"Romantic Reruns." *Ms.,* August 1979, 60–62, 68–72.
"She Knew What She Wanted." *Redbook,* February 1986, 44–51, 152–53.
"Simple Truth, The." *Ms.,* July 1978, 73–75.
"Small Losses." *Seventeen,* June 1979, 150–51.
"Summer Folk." *Ms.*, April 1981, 69, 71–73, 82–83.

"You Will Be Missed." *Commonweal,* December 19, 2014, 13–19.

ESSAYS

"The Annual Sermon, Retold." *New York Times,* December 25, 1997. https://www.nytimes.com/1997/12/25/opinion/the-annual-sermon-retold.html (accessed August 23, 2018).

"ART: Dark Domestic Visions? So What Else Is New?" *New York Times,* October 13, 1991, Sunday Book Review. https://www.nytimes.com/1991/10/13/arts/art-dark-domestic-visions-so-what-else-is-new.html (accessed August 23, 2018).

"*Bend Sinister:* A Handbook for Writers." In *Sewanee Writers on Writing,* edited by Wyatt Prunty. 125–37. Baton Rouge: Louisiana State University Press, 2000.

"Books and Babies." In *Women, Creativity, and the Arts: Critical and Autobiographical Perspectives,* edited by Diane Apostolos-Cappadona and Lucinda Ebersole. 196–98. New York: Continuum, 1997.

"Christmas Critics." *Commonweal,* December 7, 2007, 26–27.

"Confessions of a Reluctant Catholic." *Commonweal,* February 11, 2000, 12–16.

"In Praise of the Great Teachers: Three Students Recall Lessons of a Lifetime." *Washington Post,* November 6, 1994, R1.

"The Lunatic in the Pew: Confessions of a Natural-Born Catholic." *Boston College Magazine,* Summer 2003. http://bcm.bc.edu/issues/summer_2003/ft_natural.html (accessed August 23, 2018).

"Night without End, Amen; What Was One Shuddering Fan Sucking the Heat out of the House, When All of Manhattan Was Pumping It Back In Again." *Washington Post Magazine,* July 12, 1998, W11.

"The Old Haunts." *New York Times Magazine,* September 6, 2013, 66.

"Only Connect." *Sewanee Review* 125 no. 2 (Spring 2017): 420–43.

"Our Literary Wake." In "Final Rewards: The Place of Death and Mourning in Contemporary Life." *America,* March 14, 2016, 14–18.

"Redeemed from Death? The Faith of a Catholic Novelist." *Commonweal,* May 3, 2013, 14–16.

"Revelation." *Commonweal,* December 3, 2010, 30.

"Ten-Age [*sic*] Films: Love, Death and the Prom." *New York Times,* August 16, 1987. http://www.nytimes.com/1987/08/16/movies/ten-age-films-love-death-and-the-prom.html (accessed August 23, 2018).

"What (and Why) Mothers Always Know." *Washington Post,* May 10, 1998, C01.

FOREWORDS

Foreword to *City Lights: Stories about New York,* by Dan Barry. xiii–xvi. New York: St. Martin's Press, 2007.

Foreword to *Up All Night: Practical Wisdom for Mothers and Fathers,* edited by Gregory Orfalea and Barbara Rosewicz. xi–xiv. New York / Mahwah, NJ: Paulist Press, 2004.

BOOK REVIEWS

"Back Home to Carolina." Review of *Tending to Virginia,* by Jill McCorkle. *New York Times,* October 11, 1987. http://nytimes.com/1987/10/11/books/back-home-to-caroina.html (accessed August 21, 2018).

"Crazed Protagonist Deranges Novel." Review of *Brain Fever,* by Dorothy Sayers. *Commonweal,* June 1, 1996, 20–21.

"Gangsters and Pranksters." Review of *The Mysteries of Pittsburgh,* by Michael Chabon. *New York Times,* April 3. 1988, Sunday Book Review. http://www.nytimes.com/1988/04/03/books/gangsters-and-pranksters.html (accessed August 21, 2108).

"The Girl Columbus Discovered." Review of *Morning Girl,* by Michael Dorris. *New York Times Book Review,* November 8, 1992, Sunday Book Review. http://www.nytimes.com/1992/11/08/books/children-s-books-the-girl-columbus-discovered.html (accessed August 21, 2018).

"Home Alone." Review of *Amber Was Brave, Essie Was Smart,* by Vera B. Williams. *New York Times,* November 18, 2001. http://www.nytimes.com/search?endDate=20020101&query=Amber%20was%20brave&sort=best&startDate=20010101 (accessed August 21, 2018).

"In the Vicarage." Review of *Bad Blood,* by Lorna Sage. *Commonweal,* August 16, 2002, 23–24.

"Ravishing Witch, Ph.D." Review of *Half Moon Street,* by Paul Theroux. *New York Times,* October 28, 1984, Sunday Book Review. http://www.nytimes.com/1984/10/28/books/ravishing-witch-phd.html (accessed August 21, 2018).

"A Riot of Loving, Longing, Finding." Review of *Four Letters of Love,* by Niall Williams. *Commonweal,* December 19, 1997, 18–19.

"A Sense of the Miraculous." Review of *The Patron Saint of Liars,* by Ann Patchett. *New York Times,* July 26, 1992, Sunday Book Review. http://www.nytimes.com/1992/07/26/books/a-sense-of-the-miraculous.html (accessed August 21, 2108).

"Stuffed in a Fantasy." Review of *H,* by Elizabeth Shepard. *New York Times,* April 9, 1995, Sunday Book Review. http://nytimes.com/1995/04/09/books/stuffed-in-a-fantasy.html (accessed August 21, 2018).

"A Tapestry of Life, Woven in Words." Review of *Kaaterskill Falls,* by Allegra Goodman. *Commonweal,* November 6, 1998, 16–17.

"Tee Wee Tator and Flytrap Klinkenburg." Review of *Our House: The Stories of Levittown,* by Pam Conrad. Illustrated by Brian Selznick. *New York Times,* November 12, 1995, Sunday Book Review. http://www.nytimes.com/1995/11/12/books/tee-wee-tator-and-flytrap-klinkenburg.html (accessed August 21, 2018).

"Tragedy in Ireland." Review of *The Story of Lucy Gault,* by William Trevor. *Atlantic Monthly,* October 2002, 157–58.

"What Little Girls Are Made Of." Review of *Cat's Eye,* by Margaret Atwood. *New York Times,* February 2, 1989, Sunday Book Review. http://www.nytimes.com/1989/02/05/books/what-little-girls-are-made-of.html (accessed August 21, 2018).

"Whodunit?" Review of *When We Were Orphans,* by Kazuo Ishiguro. *Commonweal,* November 3, 2000, 25–26.

"A Woman's Troubles." Review of *Stone Heart,* by Luanne Rice. *New York Times,* July 1, 1990, Sunday Book Review. https://www.nytimes.com/1990/07/01/books/a-woman-s-troubles.html (accessed August 21, 2018).

INTERVIEWS, PANEL DISCUSSIONS, LECTURES

Abood, Maureen. "Between the Lines." *U.S. Catholic* 72 no. 3 (March 2007): 24–28.

"Alice McDermott." Interview with Katherine U. Henderson. In *Inter/View: Talks with America's Writing Women,* edited by Mickey Pearlman and Katherine U. Henderson, 95–101. Lexington: University Press of Kentucky, 2015.

Contino, Paul J. "A Conversation with Alice McDermott." *Image: A Journal of the Arts and Religion* 52 (2007): 61–72.

"Conversation between Alice McDermott and Thomas Lynch on Death and Grieving in Our Culture Today." Americamagazine.org, March 4, 2016. http://www.americamagazine.org/arts-culture/2016/03/04/conversation-between-alice-mcdermott-and-thomas-lynch-death-and-grieving (accessed August 23, 2018).

Dellasega, Cheryl. "Mothers Who Write: Alice McDermott." *Internet Writing Journal,* September 2002. https://www.writerswrite.com/journal/sep02/mothers-who-write-alice-mcdermott-9023 (accessed August 23, 2018).

Domestico, Anthony. "Where the Mystery Lies: An Interview with Alice McDermott." *Commonweal,* December 15, 2017, 120–23.

"An Evening with Alice McDermott '71." Interview with Mary Ellen Minogue. Sacred Heart Academy, Hempstead, New York, October 18, 2017.

Farnsworth, Elizabeth. "Alice McDermott: 'Charming Billy.'" *PBS Newshour,* November 20, 1998. http://www.pbs.org/newshour/bb/entertainment-july-dec98-mcdermott_11-20/html (accessed June 13, 2017).

Heim, Joe. "Novelist Alice McDermott on Trusting Her Readers Enough to Stay Subtle." *Washington Post,* August 7, 2015. https://www.washingtonpost.com/lifestyle/magazine/novelist-alice-mcdermott-on-what-she-owes-readers-and-not-winning-awards/2015/08/03/315bc23c-2685-11e5-b77f-eb13a215f593_story.html?utm_term=.9d3e4daeob2b (accessed August 23, 2018).

McCartin, James. "Unto Dust: A Literary Wake." October 15, 2015. https://www.youtube.com/watch?v=eEpGtS49QB4 (accessed August 23, 2018).

Osen, Diane. "Alice McDermott." In *The Book That Changed My Life: Interviews with National Book Award Winners and Finalists,* edited by Diane Osen, 109–20. Introduction by Neil Baldwin. New York: Modern Library, 2002.

Reilly, Charlie. "An Interview with Alice McDermott." *Contemporary Literature* 46, no. 4 (Winter 2005): 556–78.

Rendelstein, Jill. "Picture Perfect." *The World & I: Washington* 15, no. 3 (Mar 2000): 284–89.

Smith, Tom. "Writers Online." *Writers Online Magazine.* New York State Writers *Institute,* State University of New York, Summer 1988. http://www.albany.edu/writers-inst/webpages4/archives/olv2n3.html#mcdermott (accessed August 23, 2018).

Smith, Wendy. "Alice McDermott." *Publishers Weekly,* March 30, 1992, 85–86.

Treisman, Deborah. "This Week in Fiction: Alice McDermott." *New Yorker,* August 17, 2015. http://www.newyorker.com/books/page-turner/fiction-this-week-alice-mcdermott-2015-08-24 (accessed June 3, 2017).

Secondary Sources

Acocella, Joan. "The Children's Hour." Review of *Child of My Heart,* by Alice McDermott. *New Yorker,* November 11, 2002. Academic oneFile, http://link.galegroup.com/apps/doc/A94158137/AONE?u=nysl_li_liu&sid=AONE&xid=188a7aec (accessed June 29, 2017).

———. "Heaven's Gate." Review of *After This. New Yorker,* September 11, 2006, 83.

"Alice McDermott." Ireland House Oral History Collection, Archives of Irish America, New York University, November 12, 2010. https://www.nyu.edu/library/bobst/research/aia/collections/ihoral/mcdermotta/mcdermotta.php (accessed August 23, 2018).

"Alice McDermott." *Newsmakers.* Gale, 1999. *Biography in Context.* http://link.gale group.com/apps/doc/K1618002681/BIC?u=pwlopacplus&sid=BIC&xid=6d877b99 (accessed August 14. 2018).

Anderson, David E. "*After This* by Alice McDermott: On Mortality and a Marriage." *Religion and Ethics Weekly,* December 29, 2006. http://www.pbs.org/wnet/religionand ethics/2006/12/29/alice-mcdermott/23492/#.WWZC3uodj$c.email (accessed August 23, 2018).

Atwood, Margaret. "Castle of the Imagination." Review of *Child of My Heart,* by Alice McDermott. *New York Review of Books,* January 16, 2003, 27–29.

Balliett, Whitney. "Families." Review of *That Night,* by Alice McDermott. *New Yorker,* August 17, 1987, 17–18, 20.

Baumann, Paul. "Imperishable Identities." Review of *At Weddings and Wakes,* by Alice McDermott. *Commonweal,* May 22, 1992, 15–16.

Becker, Alida. "Oh, Where Have You Been?" Review of *Charming Billy,* by Alice McDermott. *New York Times,* January 1, 1998, Sunday Book Review. http://www.nytimes .com/1998/01/11/books/oh-where-have-you-been.html (accessed August 23, 2018).

Begley, Sarah. "Grace and Gumption in Irish-Catholic Brooklyn." Review of *The Ninth Hour,* by Alice McDermott. *Time,* October 2, 2017.

Bolotin, Craig, dir. *That Night,* 1992; Burbank, Calif.: Alcor Films/Warner Brothers.

Brown, Rosellen. "Adolescent Angst." Review of *That Night,* by Alice McDermott. *Ms.,* May 1987, 17–18, 20.

Carden, Mary Paniccia. "'Kingdom by the Sea': Romantic Histories, Vacant Futures, and Alice McDermott's Post-September 11th Lament." *CLIO: A Journal of Literature, History, and the Philosophy of History* 37, no. 2 (2008): 239–59.

———. "Making Love, Making History: (Anti)Romance in Alice McDermott's *At Weddings and Wakes* and *Charming Billy.*" In *Doubled Plots: Romance and History,* edited by Susan Strehle and Mary Paniccia Carden. 3–23. Jackson: University Press of Mississippi, 2003.

Charles, Ron. "Alice McDermott on Being a Novelist and a Believer." *Washington Post,* May 19, 2014. http://www.washingtonpost.com/news/arts-and-entertainment/wp/ 2014/05/18/alice-mcdermott-on-being-a-novelist-and-a-believer/?utm_term=.e1 (accessed August 23, 2018).

Cohen, Leah Hager. "The Drift of Years." Review of *Someone,* by Alice McDermott. *New York Times,* September 6, 2013, Sunday Book Review. https://www.nytimes .com/2013/09/08/books/review/someone-by-alice-mcdermott.html (accessed August 21, 2108).

Contino, Paul J. "Caught at the Crossroads." Review of *After This,* by Alice McDermott. *America,* October 9, 2006, 26–29.

———. "Gleams of Life Everlasting in Alice McDermott's *Someone.*" *Christianity and Literature* 63, no. 4 (Summer 2014): 503–11.

Cooper, Rand Richards. "Charming Alice: A Unique Voice in American Fiction." *Commonweal* March 27, 1998, 10–12.

Corso, Gail S. "Allie, Phoebe, Robert Emmet, and Daisy Mae: Love, Loss, and Grief in J. D. Salinger's *The Catcher in the Rye* and Alice McDermott's *Child of My Heart.*" *Teaching American Literature: A Journal of Theory and Practice* 8, no. 3 (Fall 2016): 92–111.

———. "Psychoanalysing Theresa: Telling It Slant in Alice McDermott's *Child of My Heart*." *Studies in Arts and Humanities* 3, no. 1 (2017): 20–33.

Coughlan, Patricia. "Paper Ghosts: Reading the Uncanny in Alice McDermott." *Éire-Ireland* 47, nos. 1 and 2 (Spring/Summer 2012): 123–46.

Crabtree-Sinnett, Claire. "A Condition of Permanent Mourning: Resonances of Joyce in Alice McDermott's *At Weddings and Wakes* and *Charming Billy*." *British and American Studies* 18 (2012): 35–43.

———. "Piety, Innocence, and Irishness in Alice McDermott's Irish-American Novels." *Journal of Research in Gender Studies* 1, no. 1 (2011): 43–54.

Cronin, Meoghan B. "Maiden Mothers and Little Sisters: The Convent Novel Grows Up." In *Between Human and Divine: The Catholic Vision in Contemporary Literature,* edited by Mary R. Reichardt, 262–80. Washington, D.C.: Catholic University of America Press, 2010.

Crowe, David. "*The Ninth Hour:* A Novel." Review of *The Ninth Hour,* by Alice McDermott. *Christian Century,* April 11, 2018.

Cummings, Alex Sayf. "Trying to Be Someone in Irish, Working-Class Brooklyn: Alice McDermott's *Someone*." *Tropics of Meta,* October 15, 2013. https://tropicsofmeta.wordpress.com/2013/10/15/trying-to-be-someone-in-irish-working-class-brooklyn-alice-mcdermotts-someone (accessed June 13, 2017).

Deignan, Tom. "Alice McDermott's 'After' World." Review of *After This,* by Alice McDermott. *Irish Voice,* September 20, 2006, 23.

———. "The CRAIC: Alice McDermott; Reluctantly Irish?" *Irish Voice,* December 14, 1999, 17.

———. "Take Another Piece of My 'Heart.'" Review of *Child of My Heart,* by Alice McDermott. *Irish Voice,* January 14, 2003, 24.

———. "A World Away." Review of *Child of My Heart,* by Alice McDermott, *America,* February 17, 2003.

Diner, Hasia R. *Erin's Daughters in America: Irish Immigrant Women in the Nineteenth Century.* London: Johns Hopkins University Press, 1983.

Doyle, Brian. "After This." Review of *After This,* by Alice McDermott. *Christian Century,* February 20, 2007, 49–51.

Ebest, Sally Barr. "'Reluctant Catholics': Contemporary Irish-American Women Writers." In *The Catholic Church and Unruly Women Writers: Critical Essays,* edited by Jeana DelRosso, Leigh Eicke, and Ana Kothe, 159–73. New York: Palgrave Macmillan, 2007.

———. "These Traits Also Endure: Contemporary Irish and Irish-American Women Writers." *New Hibernia Review* 7, no. 2 (Summer 2003): 55–72.

Eder, Richard. "Letting a Little Air In." Review of *At Weddings and Wakes,* by Alice McDermott. *Los Angeles Times Book Review,* April 12, 1992, 3, 7.

———. Review of *That Night, Los Angeles Times Book Review,* April 26, 1987. http://articles.latimes.com/1987-04-26/books/bk-1318_1_alice-mcdermott.

Ellin, Ally. "The Gloves Are Definitely Gone at the Katharine Gibbs Schools," *New York Times,* September 15, 2002, https://www.nytimes.com/2002/09/15/jobs/the-gloves-are-definitely-gone-at-the-katharine-gibbs-schools.html (accessed August 24, 2018).

Ganeshram, Ramin. "A Long-Ago Island Inspires Her Fiction." Review of *Child of My Heart,* by Alice McDermott. *New York Times,* February 23, 2003. http://www.nytimes.com/2003/02/23/nyregion/arts-entertainment-a-long-ago-island-inspires-her-fiction.html (accessed August 21, 2018).

Gioia, Dana. "The Catholic Writer Today." *First Things,* December 2013. https://www.firstthings.com/article/2013/12/the-catholic-writer-today (accessed August 23, 2018).

Gordon, Mary. "In Alice McDermott's Novel, A Cloistered Life Blows Open." Review of *The Ninth Hour,* by Alice McDermott. *New York Times,* October 2, 2017. http://www.nytimes.com/2017/10/02/books/review/the-ninth-hour-alice-mcdermott.html (accessed August 21, 2018).

Gorra, Michael. "Cottage Industry: Alice McDermott's Heroine, A Baby Sitter for the Summer, Comes of Age on Long Island." Review of *Child of My Heart,* by Alice McDermott. *New York Times,* November 24, 2002. http://www.nytimes.com/2002/11/24/books/cottage-industry.html (accessed August 21, 2018).

Gray, Paul. "Family Album," review of *After This,* by Alice McDermott, *New York Times,* September 10, 2006, Sunday Book Review, http://www.nytimes.com/2006/09/10/books/review/gray.html (accessed August 21, 2018).

Hagan, Edward A. "The American Wake: Alice McDermott, *Child of My Heart.*" In *Goodbye Yeats and O'Neill: Farce in Contemporary Irish and Irish-American Narratives,* 191–203. Amsterdam: Rodopi, 2010.

Haile, Beth. "Can Every Sin Be Forgiven?" *U.S. Catholic,* September 2017, 49.

Hallissy, Margaret. "Bringing Paddies Over: Alice McDermott's *Charming Billy.*" In *Reading Irish-American Fiction: The Hyphenated Self,* 127–47. New York: Palgrave Macmillan, 2006.

Harvey, Clodagh Brennan. *Contemporary Irish Traditional Narrative: The English Language Tradition.* Folklore and Mythology Studies 35. Berkeley: University of California Press, 1992.

Harvey, Stephen. Review of *A Bigamist's Daughter,* by Alice McDermott. *Village Voice,* February 23, 1982, 43.

Homer. *Odyssey*, translated by Stanley Lombardo. In *The Norton Anthology of Western Literature,* ed. Martin Puchner et al., 9th ed., vol. 1. New York: W. W. Norton, 2014.

Jacobson, Beatrice. "Alice McDermott's Narrators." In *Too Smart to be Sentimental: Contemporary Irish American Women Writers,* edited by Sally Barr Ebest and Kathleen McInerny, 116–35. Notre Dame, Ind.: University of Notre Dame Press, 2008.

Jones, Malcolm. "All Sugar, No Spice." Review of *Child of My Heart,* by Alice McDermott, *Newsweek,* November 18, 2002.

Jurca, Catherine. "The White Diaspora." In *White Diaspora: The Suburb and the Twentieth-Century American Novel,* 3–19. Princeton, N.J.: Princeton University Press, 2001.

Kakutani, Michiko. "The Lessons of Loss Learned in Childhood." Review of *At Weddings and Wakes,* by Alice McDermott. *New York Times,* March 24, 1992. http://www.nytimes.com/1992/03/24/books/books-of-the-times-the-lessons-of-loss-learned-in-childhood.html (accessed August 21, 2018).

———. "Lost Illusions." Review of *That Night,* by Alice McDermott. *New York Times,* March 28, 1987. http://www.nytimes.com/1987/03/28/books/books-of-the-times-lost-illusions.html (accessed August 21, 2018).

Kane, T. C., and J. F. Tuohey. "Suicide." *New Catholic Encyclopedia,* 2nd ed., 13:598–99. Detroit: Gale, 2003.

King, Lily. "Alice McDermott's New Novel Begins with Suicide and Culminates in Murder."

Washington Post, September 14, 2017. https://www.washingtonpost.com/entertainment/books/alice-mcdermotts-new-novel-begins-with-suicide-and-culminates-in-murder/2017/

09/14/dde9b18a-94ce-11e7-aace-04b862b2b3f3_story.html?utm_term=.2a933b72ff6f (accessed August 23, 2018).

Klinkenborg, Verlyn. "Grief That Lasts Forever." Review of *At Weddings and Wakes,* by Alice McDermott. *New York Times,* April 12, 1992, Sunday Book Review. http://www.nytimes.com/1992/04/12/books/grief-that-lasts-forever.html (accessed August 21, 2018).

Lauder, Robert E. "After Alice: The Emergence of a New Kind of Catholic Novel." *America,* October 5, 2009. https://www.americamagazine.org/arts-culture/2009/10/05/after-alice-emergence-new-kind-catholic-novel (accessed August 23, 2018).

Leavitt, David. "Fathers, Daughters, and Hoodlums." Review of *That Night,* by Alice McDermott, *New York Times,* April 19, 1987, http://www.nytimes.com/1987/04/19/books/fathers-daughters-and-hoodlums.html (accessed August 21, 2018).

Lewis, John. "Class Act: Acclaimed Author Alice McDermott Is Also Revered in Her Johns Hopkins Classroom," *Baltimore Magazine,* March 13, 2004, https://baltimoremagazine.com/2014/3/13/acclaimed-author-alice-mcdermott-is-also-revered-in-her-johns-hopkins-classroom (accessed August 23, 2018).

López, Lorraine M. "Reverberant Music in *After This.*" *Southern Review* 43, no. 1 (Winter 2007): 237–40.

Lysaght, Patricia. *A Pocket Book of the Banshee.* Dublin: O'Brien, 1998.

Maslin, Janet. "Survivor among a Lifetime of Ghosts." Review of *Someone,* by Alice McDermott. *New York Times,* October 7, 2013. http://www.nytimes.com/2013/10/07/books/alice-mcdermotts-new-novel-someone.html (accessed August 21, 2018).

McAlpin, Heller. "In *The Ninth Hour,* A Tonic for the Ills of the World." *NPR,* September 21, 2017. http://www.npr.org/2017/09/21/548665244/in-the-ninth-hour-a-tonic-for-the-ills-of-the-world (accessed August 23, 2018).

McGlynn, Jenny. "Gush of Wind as Omen of Death." In "Legends of the Supernatural," *Field Day Anthology of Irish Writing,* vol. 4: *Irish Women's Writing and Traditions,* edited by Angela Bourke, 1309. Cork: Cork University Press, 2002.

Meyer, Eugene L. "Writer Alice McDermott's Themes Are Universal." *Washington Post,* September 9, 2013. http://www.washingtonpost.com/entertainment/books/writer-alice-mcdermotts-themes-are-universal/2013/09/09/f1aabdf2-14c3-11e3-880b-7503237cc69d_story.html?utm_term=.891607b29276 (accessed August 23, 2018).

Miller, Kerby A. *Emigrants and Exiles: Ireland and the Irish Exodus to North America.* New York: Oxford University Press, 1985.

Miner, Valerie. "Mixed Memories: *Night Talk* by Elizabeth Cox; *Charming Billy* by Alice McDermott." *Women's Review of Books,* July 1998, 31–32.

Moynihan, Sinéad. "'None of Us Will Always Be Here': Whiteness, Loss, and Alice McDermott's *At Weddings and Wakes.*" *Contemporary Women's Writing* 4, no. 1 (March 2010): 40–54.

Murphy, Maureen. "Bridie, We Hardly Knew Ye: The Irish Domestics." In *The Irish in America,* edited by Michael Coffey, with text by Terry Golway. 141–45. New York: Hyperion, 1997.

Myers, Marc. "Novelist Alice McDermott: Getting Courage from 'Cats'; The Author on How the Song 'Memory' Helped Push Her Forward Early in Her Career." *Wall Street Journal (Online),* September 26, 2017.

Myers, Nathan. "'Too Much Yeats': Alice McDermott's *Charming Billy* and an Irish Poet's American Legacy." *Papers on Language and Literature* 52, no. 2 (Spring 2016): 149–76.

Nolan, Janet A. *Ourselves Alone: Women's Emigration from Ireland, 1885–1920*. Lexington: University Press of Kentucky, 1989.

O'Connell, Michael. "'The Glorious Impossible': Belief and Ambiguity in the Fiction of Alice McDermott." *Religion and the Arts* 20 (2016): 491–506.

O'Connell, Shaun. "Home and Away: Imagining Ireland Imagining America (2013)." *New England Journal of Public Policy* 28, no. 1 (2015): article 15.

———. "That Much Credit: Irish-American Identity and Writing." *Massachusetts Review* 44, nos. 1 and 2 (Spring–Summer 2003): 251–68.

O'Gorman, Farrell. "Between Human and Divine: The Catholic Vision in Contemporary Literature." *Christianity and Literature* 61, no. 2 (Winter 2012): 343–47.

O'Reilly, Mollie Wilson. "Nothing to Be Done?" Review of *The Ninth Hour,* by Alice McDermott. *Commonweal,* November 10, 2017.

Phelan, J. Greg. "The Holy Fool." Review of *Someone,* by Alice McDermott. *America,* November 25, 2013, 28–30.

Podhoretz, John. "Disappointing Alice." Review of *Child of My Heart,* by Alice McDermott. *The Weekly Standard: Washington,* December 9, 2002, 31–33.

Preziosi, Dominic, "A Bold Piece." Review of *Someone,* by Alice McDermott. *Commonweal,* November 15, 2013, 31–32.

Quinn, Peter. "Clement and Loving." Review of *After This,* by Alice McDermott. *Commonweal,* October 20, 2006, 25–27.

———. *Looking for Jimmy: A Search for Irish America.* Woodstock, N.Y.: Overlook Press, 2007.

Ripatrazone, Nick. "Binding Wounds." Review of *The Ninth Hour,* by Alice McDermott. *National Review,* October 16, 2017, 55–56.

Roberts, Roxanne. "The Accidental Novelist: Bethesda's Alice McDermott and Her Latest Reluctant Success." *Washington Post,* April 21, 1992. http://www.highbeam.com/doc/1P2-1001926.html (accessed August 23, 2018).

Rothstein, Mervyn. "The Storyteller Is Part of the Tale." Review of *That Night,* by Alice McDermott. *New York Times,* May 9, 1987. http://nytimes.com/1987/05/09/books/the-storyteller-is-part-of-the-tale.html (accessed August 21, 2018).

Schnapp, Patricia L. "Shades of Redemption in Alice McDermott's Novels." In *Between Human and Divine: The Catholic Vision in Contemporary Literature,* edited by Mary Reichardt. 15–31. Washington, D.C.: Catholic University of America Press, 2010.

Shank, Jenny. "In the Old Neighborhoods of Brooklyn, Sister Knows Best." Review of *The Ninth Hour,* by Alice McDermott. *America,* September 18, 2017.

Shannon, William V. *The American Irish.* New York: Macmillan, 1963.

Simpson, Mona. "Coming of Age on Long Island." Review of *Child of My Heart,* by Alice McDermott. *Atlantic Monthly,* December 2002, 153.

Steinfels, Margaret O'Brien. "The Age of Innocence." Review of *Child of My Heart,* by Alice McDermott. *Commonweal,* January 31, 2003, 28–29.

———. "The Archeology of Yearning: Alice McDermott." *U.S. Catholic Historian* 23, no. 3 (Summer 2005): 93–107.

Third Plenary Council of Baltimore, *A Catechism of Christian Doctrine,* 1895, Project Gutenberg, www.gutenberg.org/files/14552/14552.txt.

Thurston, Anne. "Honouring the Ordinary: A Reflection on the Novel *After This* by Alice McDermott." *Furrow* 58, no. 10 (October 2007): 537–40.

Tyler, Anne. "Novels by Three Emerging Writers." Review of *A Bigamist's Daughter,*

New York Times, February 21, 1982, Sunday Book Review, https://www.nytimes.com/1982/02/21/books/novels-by-three-emerging-writers-249593.html.

Vejvoda, Kathleen. "'Too Much Knowledge of the Other World': Women and Nineteenth-Century Irish Folktales." *Victorian Literature and Culture* 32, no. 1 (April 14, 2004): 41–61.

Watkins, Karen Ahlefelder. "A Streetcar Named Syosset." Review of *That Night,* by Alice McDermott. *New Republic,* May 25, 1987, 37–38.

Wolfe, Gregory. "The Catholic Writer, Then and Now." *Image: A Journal of the Arts and Religion* 79 (Fall 2014): 3–6.

INDEX